CELEBRATING
THE FEASTS OF ISRAEL

Second Expanded Edition

Explore the Depth of Our Faith in Jesus
Christ and Pass It on to the Next Generation

To Michael
Blessings - Werner Sonderegger

WERNER SONDEREGGER

ISBN 978-1-64492-876-9 (paperback)
ISBN 978-1-64515-774-8 (hardcover)
ISBN 978-1-64492-877-6 (digital)

Christian Faith Publishing, Inc.
832 Park Avenue
Meadville, PA 16335
www.christianfaithpublishing.com

Printed in the United States of America

CONTENTS

FOREWORD

For the purpose of this book, the Feasts of Israel are placed in two categories:

- "The Feasts of the Lord"—God commanded Israel to keep these.
- "The Feasts of the Jews"—God gave no command for these.

There are a great variety of feasts celebrated in the Jewish community that fall in the second category. This book examines only the ones that show significance to our faith in Jesus Christ.

Each study of the Feasts of Israel will focus on Gods command, biblical history and the feast's fulfillment in Christ, thereby revealing the significance for our Christian faith and life. In doing so, we will examine the key sacrifices, offerings, and Jewish customs that differentiate each feast. Several specific Bible teachings and testimonies are added to capture the richness of the feasts in our personal growth and relationship with Christ.

I recommend writing down whatever God speaks to your heart, along with any insights you might have.

Each "Practical Guide" portion will suggest ways to meaningfully celebrate these feasts in your Christian families. It will serve as a wonderful tool to show how we can pass on our faith in Jesus Christ to the next generation.

Great attention is given so that the Bible translation utilized for particular sequences of teaching is simple and clear. You find therefore a variety of translations used:

- KJV: King James Version
- NKJV: New King James Version
- NASB: New American Standard Bible
- NLT: New Living Translation
- ESV: English Standard Version

CHAPTER 1

DANGER / PREFACE

Walking in the Footsteps of Jesus

Your life is about to change! Are you wondering why? Continue to find out. Let's take a little journey back in time. Imagine yourself living in a small peaceful village nestled in the countryside about a day's journey from Jerusalem. The time is 20 BC. Are you ready?

Today is not an ordinary day. You are eager to begin your journey from your hometown village to Jerusalem. There you are now walking along the way and bringing with you a lamb out of your flock. You chose this particular lamb only after careful observation and inspection. Your eyes did not find one single blemish.

However, there is something heavy in your heart. You feel convicted and guilty of having sinned by unintentionally breaking one of God's commandments. You had condemned yourself for being so foolish. But now you have a new sense of hope and are looking forward to your arrival at the temple in Jerusalem. You made up your mind to obey God's command for such situations—bring a lamb without blemish as a sin offering. God explained in Leviticus, "For the life of the body is in its blood. I have given you the blood on the altar to purify you, making you right with the LORD. It is the blood, given in exchange for a life, that makes purification possible" (Leviticus 17:11).

As you walk along the way you look down at your lamb. Your eyes meet. Yet the silence is only interrupted by a soft "baa." Your thoughts are captivated by what will happen in the temple. Finally, after many hours have passed, you arrive. God had very specifically described in His command how your lamb needed to be sacrificed. You cannot just drop the lamb off at the temple as if writing a check for the debt you owe. No, not at all! You personally will go to the priest.

The priest will not kill the lamb for you. No, you will. God instructed that you place your hands—and by that, your sins—on the head of the innocent and blameless lamb. Then you pierce it to its death. Only then will the priest take some of the blood of the lamb with his finger and put it on the horns of the altar of burnt offerings. He will pour out the rest of the blood at the base of the altar. The fat of the lamb he will remove and burn on the altar as a pleasing aroma to the Lord. In doing these things, the priest will make atonement for you and your sin which you have committed, and you shall be forgiven.

Text: Leviticus 4:27–35

Let's go even further back in time when Israel was held enslaved in Egypt. Again there is a lamb sacrificed without any defect. It became to be the first Passover Feast.

> And they shall take some of the blood (lamb)
> and put it on the two doorposts and on the lintel
> of the houses where they eat it. (Exodus 12:7)

> For the LORD will pass through to strike
> the Egyptians; and when He sees the blood (of
> the Passover lamb) on the lintel and on the two
> doorposts, the LORD will pass over the door and
> not allow the destroyer to come into your houses
> to strike you. (Exodus 12:23)

You will find that John speaks about a Passover lamb in the New Testament. He calls Jesus the Lamb of God.

> The next day, John saw Jesus coming toward
> him, and said, "Behold! The Lamb of God who
> takes away the sin of the world!" (John 1:29)

Jesus Christ became our Passover lamb. The penalty for our sins was paid by the blood He shed for us on the cross.

> God did by sending his own Son in the likeness of sinful man to be a sin offering. (Romans 8:3)

Do you remember your visit in the temple? The lamb of your sin offering? Interesting that you personally laid your hands on the head of the lamb and by it your sin and then killed it. And now we are seeing Jesus Christ having before his crucifixion a crown of thorns placed upon his head. Like it was by your sin offering, you are personally called to come to the cross, to Jesus Christ, the Lamb of God. It was your sins that Christ carried and by his death paid the penalty for it on the cross. Why, you may ask?

> For God so loved the world that He gave His only begotten Son, that whoever believes in Him should not perish but have everlasting life. For God did not send His son into the world to condemn the world, but that the world through Him might be saved. (John 3:16–17)

> Therefore, we who have fled to him for refuge can have great confidence as we hold to the hope that lies before us. This hope is a strong and trustworthy anchor for our souls. It leads us through the curtain into God's inner sanctuary. Jesus has already gone in there for us. He has become our eternal High Priest in the order of Melchizedek. (Hebrew 6:18–20)

The Feasts of Israel are in essence the story of Jesus Christ, your messiah. Come along by walking in the footsteps of Jesus through the Bible. The feasts were a foreshadowing of things to come. Christ Himself is the substance of this shadow. They also carry God's marvelous plan for you. Pray as you read. Meditate on each Bible reference to dig deeper in God's word. Don't lose what God reveals and speaks to you. Write it down.

Jesus explained:

> I am the light of the world. If you follow me,
> you won't have to walk in darkness, because you
> will have the light that leads to life. (John 8:12)

We Christians are called to be a light in this world. Christ in you is that light. Wherever you are today, simply by your presence, the darkness knows it is in danger because of your willingness to follow Christ. Why, you may ask? Listen.

> I (Jesus Christ) am sending you to the Gentiles to open their eyes, so they may turn from darkness to light and from the power of Satan to God. Then they will receive forgiveness for their sins and be given a place among God's people, who are set apart by faith in me. (Acts 26:17–18)

> Then Jesus again spoke to them, saying, "I am the Light of the world; he who follows Me will not walk in the darkness, but will have the Light of life." (John 8:12)

> Above all, you must live as citizens of heaven, conducting yourselves in a manner worthy of the Good News about Christ. Then, whether I come and see you again or only hear about you, I will know that you are standing together with one spirit and one purpose, fighting together for the faith, which is the Good News. (Philippians 1:27)

> Fight the good fight for the true faith. Hold tightly to the eternal life to which God has called

you, which you have declared so well before many witnesses. (1 Timothy 6:12)

> I have fought the good fight, I have finished the race, and I have remained faithful. (2 Timothy 4:7)

Go boldly forward. Listen to the words of Paul:

> I fall to my knees and pray to the Father, the Creator of everything in heaven and on earth. I pray that from his glorious, unlimited resources he will empower you with inner strength through his Spirit. Then Christ will make his home in your hearts as you trust in him. Your roots will grow down into God's love and keep you strong. And may you have the power to understand, as all God's people should, how wide, how long, how high, and how deep his love is. May you experience the love of Christ, though it is too great to understand fully. Then you will be made complete with all the fullness of life and power that comes from God. (Ephesians 3:14–19)

My passion and prayer for you is that you experience your faith in Christ as a joyful fountain of life. Receive a new revelation about the solid rock you have built your faith on. He is with you! Take some time with God to reflect on the following song.

He Looked Beyond My Fault
by Dottie Rambo

Amazing grace shall always be my song of praise,
for it was grace that brought my liberty;
I do not know just why He came to love me so,
He looked beyond my fault and saw my need.

I shall forever lift mine eyes to Calvary,
to view the cross where Jesus died for me,
how marvelous the grace that caught my falling
    soul;
He looked beyond my fault and saw my need.
I shall forever lift mine eyes to Calvary,
to view the cross where Jesus died for me,
how marvelous the grace that caught my falling
    soul;
He looked beyond my fault and saw my need.

CHAPTER 2

THE FEASTS OF THE LORD
These Are the Feasts Commanded by God

The feasts of the Lord are identified as the ones God commanded the Israelites to celebrate. We will later focus on some festivals (The Feasts of the Jews) which have significance for us as Christians, but are not commanded by God. This is similar to certain celebrations in today's Christian community, such as the tradition of celebrating Christmas or Easter. It might be a shocking thought for you that, in fact, Jesus Christ did not command us to celebrate these feasts. He did tell us, however, to celebrate the Lord's Supper.

> For I pass on to you what I received from the Lord himself. On the night when he was betrayed, the Lord Jesus took some bread and gave thanks to God for it. Then he broke it in pieces and said, "This is my body, which is given for you. Do this to remember me." In the same way, he took the cup of wine after supper, saying, "This cup is the new covenant between God and his people—an agreement confirmed with my blood. Do this to remember me as often as you drink it." For every time you eat this bread and drink this cup, you are announcing the Lord's death until he comes again. (1 Corinthians 11:23–26)

The Lord's Supper

I believe that we indeed have reason to celebrate Christmas and Easter with great joy. Having said this, I fervently urge you to celebrate in a way that gives all the honor to God, and expresses our undivided thankfulness and worship to Him alone.

All the feasts of the Lord were given to the Israelites by God. Each feast bears God's specific instructions regarding exactly how and when to celebrate. These feast days are the Lord's appointed festivals. God had the Israelites proclaim these days as official days for holy assembly. These were additional Sabbath days, and like all other days, they began at sundown. It was mandatory for all male Israelites to travel three times a year to God's temple in Jerusalem to celebrate these feasts.

Text: Exodus 12, 20:1–21, 31:12–18; Leviticus 23; Deuteronomy 5:12–18

The Sabbath
Introduction

Sabbath Candle

What did God have in mind when He made the feast days as additional Sabbath days? The Sabbath or *Shabbat* (Hebrew) is a special day in Judaism. *Sabbath* means rest. Along with circumcision, these two are the sign and seal of the Old Covenant. God commanded that no ordinary work is to be done on this day. It was a day of rest, commemorating the rest of God in creation. The Sabbath is part of the Ten Commandments and of the feasts. Any violation of this day would be judged by death.

Jesus lived under the Old Covenant but fulfilled it with His shed blood on the cross. He gave us a New Covenant.

Matthew 26:27, "then he took the cup, and gave thanks, and gave it to them, saying, Drink from it, all of you. For this is my blood of the new covenant, which is shed for many for the remission of sins."

The Sabbath pointed to Jesus Christ in whom we as believers find redemption and the true rest of God.

In Judaism, the Sabbath is the most important day of the week. They even refer to it as the "queen." Today, every Friday at sunset, Jews welcome the Sabbath with prayers and readings from the Torah in the synagogue. They will continue the Sabbath celebration in their homes with songs and a festive dinner, which typically includes challah bread, wine, and the Sabbath candles. This special dinner closes with a thanksgiving prayer. It is full of rich tradition and ritual.

> **INSIGHT**
>
> The Sabbath is observed from Friday evening to Saturday evening. In Judaism, Sabbath is the seventh day of the Hebrew calendar week, in English known as Saturday.

Sabbath or Sunday?

What day should we Christians celebrate; the Sabbath or Sunday? It is a question of covenant. Under the Old Covenant with the law; it is the Sabbath. Christians are under the New Covenant. The old is fulfilled. Christians also have a sign and seal of covenant, which is the baptism of the Holy Spirit. The Lord's Day or Sunday is a voluntary day of worship. It marks the day of Jesus's resurrection; the completion of our redemption and of the pouring out of the Holy Spirit at Pentecost.

Text: Isaiah 28:9–11; Acts 2:1–4; Galatians 4:10–11; Colossians 2:11, 17–18

Sabbath
Practical Guide
Celebrating The Sabbath (Simplified Version)

Sabbath starts at sundown on Friday eve. Have a festive dinner table set with some candles (Sabbath candles). It is customary that the mother along with the oldest daughter light the candles. The mother prays a prayer of blessing. Next, the mother and father may honor each other by expressing how thankful they are for each other by using some specific situations. Sing a song of praise. A prayer of blessing is spoken by the father before he serves the wine. Your son will love to be a part of this.

Next is the traditional hand washing. Pass a pitcher of water with a basin and a towel from person to person. Every Sabbath dinner needs to have some challah bread that is typically covered by a special cloth napkin at the table. Pass the challah bread and enjoy the dinner.

Traditional Sabbath Celebration

Lighting of the Sabbath Candle

The following steps and prayers are from Messianic Jewish traditions for the Sabbath. Remember, these are not laws. The intention is to give you a jump start for your own family traditions and prayers as you look and listen to Jesus Christ.

1. Blessing of the Sabbath Candle

The Sabbath candles are lit by the woman of the house before sundown on Friday. After she lights the candles, she waves her hands over the flames three times as if welcoming in the Sabbath. Covering her eyes with her hands, she recites the following blessing:

> *Blessed are You, LORD our God, King of the Universe, who sanctified us with His commandments, and commanded us to be a light to the nations and who gave us Yeshua (Jesus) our Messiah the Light of the world.*

Parents and children may use this opportunity to add their own words of blessing and offer expressions of love and appreciation to each other.

2. Kiddush for Sabbath

> **INSIGHT**
>
> *Kiddush*, meaning "sanctification," is a blessing recited over wine or grape juice to sanctify the Sabbath and Jewish holidays.

Normally, the Kiddush is recited by the father of the house while holding a cup of wine. First he recites Genesis 1:31–2:3 as a declaration to bear witness that God created the world and everything in it:

> *Then God looked over all He had made, and He saw that it was very good! And evening passed and morning came, marking the sixth day. So the creation of the heavens and the earth and everything in them was completed. On the seventh day God had finished His work of creation, so He rested from all his work. And God blessed the seventh day and declared it holy, because it was the day when He rested from all His work of creation.*

After this, the father thanks God for the gift of the Sabbath day:

> *Blessed art Thou, Adonai our God, King of the Universe, who creates the true fruit of the*

*vine—Yeshua. Blessed are You, LORD, King
of the Universe, who made us holy with His
commandments and favored us, and gave us His
holy Sabbath, in love and favor, to be our heritage,
as a reminder of the Creation. It is the foremost day
of the holy festivals marking the Exodus from Egypt.
For out of all the nations You chose us and made us
holy, and You gave us Your holy Sabbath, in love
and favor, as our heritage. Blessed are You, LORD,
who sanctifies the Sabbath.*

After this blessing is recited, it is customary to give each person some wine from the Kiddush cup.

3. Blessing of the Challah

There are two loaves of challah bread on the Sabbath table symbolizing the double portion of manna which God provided on the day before the Sabbath (Friday) for the Jews while they wandered in the wilderness (Exodus 16). The two challah breads are under a cloth as a reminder that dew was all around the camp when they awoke in the desert. Together these serve as a great reminder of God's provision.

Challah Bread

A bowl of water for handwashing and a small towel are handed from one person to the next. After handwashing, the father lifts the challah loaf and says the blessing over the bread.

*Blessed are You, Lord our God, Master of
the Universe, who gives us the Living Bread from
heaven. Amen.*

The father cuts the challah bread and distributes it to those around the table.

4. The Sabbath Meal

The Sabbath meal begins. Note: Jews normally do not "say grace" before meals, but rather after they have eaten. They do not "bless" the food either but rather acknowledge that God is the one who provides for their sustenance.

5. Grace After the Meal

Blessed are you, LORD our God, Master of the Universe, who nourishes the whole world in goodness, with grace, kindness, and compassion. He gives bread to all flesh, for His mercy endures forever. And through His great goodness we have never lacked, nor will we lack food forever, for the sake of His great name. For He is God, who nourishes and sustains all, and does good to all, and prepares food for all His creatures which He created. Blessed are You, LORD, who nourishes all. Amen.

Blessed are You, LORD our God, King of the Universe, who gave to us the way of salvation through the Messiah Yeshua, blessed be He. Amen.

INSIGHT
The priest washed in the basin before entering to God's presence in the temple on behalf of Israel (Exodus 30:17–21). Some emphasis that this ritual portrays a picture that points to Jesus. Jesus Christ washed away our guilty conscience so that we can draw near to God (Hebrews 10:22).
Messianic Jews emphasizing here that the washing of our hands is intended to show gratitude to God for His sanctification of us.
In contrast, some point to Mark 7:3–16 where Jesus opposed this traditional ritual of cleansing. Note here the distinction that Jesus was speaking against a cleansing that was based on the law of the elders.

Sabbath Day / Shabbat

Remember (Mark 2:27) that the Sabbath is a gift of God to us, a time of rest and reflection, a joyful time set apart from the busy week when we can focus on what is important in our lives. Each family will be different. Here are some Saturday activity ideas to get you started:

It's family time!

- There is something special about waking up to the smell of fresh baked bread on a Saturday morning. Or how about some homemade pancakes with maple syrup? You will be surprised how much fun it is to prepare some tasty food with your children. Before you know it, your family will have some baking and cooking traditions.
- Start the day with a proclamation: Isaiah 60:1, "Arise, shine; for your light has come, And the glory of the Lord has risen upon you."
- Let God use you by having a Bible verse ready for each person in the family.
- Read, study, and discuss God's Word. Perhaps the younger children would enjoy playing a preacher. They will love it and you will be surprised what you can learn.
- Invite some friends over for a meal and enjoy a relaxed time. Be creative, play some old fashioned outdoor games with the whole crew, or maybe you can enjoy sitting around a bonfire. What a great place to sing some praise and worship songs.

The Havdalah Ceremony[1]

This Jewish ceremony marks the symbolic end of the Shabbat and ushers in the new week. Shabbat ends on Saturday night after the appearance of the first three stars in the sky.

1. Reciting of Scripture Verses

Several verses from the Bible are recited. Example:

> *See, God has come to save me. I will trust in him and not be afraid. The Lord god is my strength and my song; he had given me victory. With joy you will drink deeply from the fountain of salvation! In that wonderful day you will sing; "Thank the Lord!*

---

[1] *Havdalah* means separation.

Praise his name! Tell the nations what he has done. Let them know how mighty he is! Sing to the Lord, for he has done wonderful things. Make known his praise around the world. Let all the people of Jerusalem shout his praise with joy! For great is the Holy One of Israel who lives among you." (Isaiah 12:2–6)

2. The Blessing Over the Wine (Kiddush)

In the same fashion as the Sabbath is welcomed with wine, so comes the Sabbath to a close with wine. The blessing is spoken, but it is not yet time to drink it. That will come at the end.

Blessing: Blessed are You, Lord our God, King of the Universe, who creates the fruit of the vine.

3. A Box of Fragrant Herbs

You will find a box of fragrant herbs at this ceremony. The smell of each individual fragrance (cloves, cinnamon, bay leaves) is to remind us of the separation from the ordinary weekdays and that of the sacred day, the Sabbath.

Blessing: Blessed are You, Lord our God, King of the Universe, creator of all spices.

4. The lighting of the Havdalah Candle. This time the candle represents light.

Genesis 1:3, "Let there be light," and there was light. And God saw that the light was good.

Hold your hand close to the flame to see a reflection on your fingernail or a shadow in your

Havdalah Candle with Spice Box

palm (see picture). It symbolizes that by this light we can work with our hands.

Blessing: Blessed are you Lord our God, King of the Universe, creator of the light of fire.

5. The Havdalah Blessing

Blessed are You, Lord our God, King of the Universe, who separates the holy from the profane, light from darkness, Israel from the nations, the seventh day from the six days of labor. Blessed are You, Lord our God, who separates the holy from the profane.

A small amount of wine from the Kiddush cup is put on a plate symbolizing the loss of the Sabbath. Then everyone drinks from the cup. And the flame of the Havdalah candle is extinguished by dipping it into the wine cup, or by dripping some of the wine onto the flame with a finger.

6. Song

Sing a song to end the Havdalah ceremony.

7. "Shave'a Tov"

In conclusion, everyone will say to one another *"Shave'a Tov,"* meaning, "a good week ahead!"

The Calendars

God said to Moses in His instruction for Passover in Egypt that it would be the first month of the year. This resulted in the sacred Jewish lunar calendar. We find three feast seasons (festivals) over a period of seven months:

- Passover is at Nisan – March / April
- Pentecost is at Sivan – May / June
- Tabernacle is at Tishrei – September / October

The feasts are held at specific times corresponding to the agricultural seasons.

Text: Exodus 12:1–2; Leviticus 23

SACRED CALENDAR	SOLAR CALENDAR	FARM SEASON	
(Lunar calendar)			
1. Nisan (Abib)	March–April	Barley Harvest	**Festival of Passover** The Omer[2]
2. Iyyar (Ziv)	April–May	Barley Harvest	
3. Sivan	May–June	Wheat Harvest	**Festival of Pentecost**
4. Tammuz	June–July	Grape Harvest	
5. Ab	July–August	Dates & Figs Harvest	
6. Elul	August–September	Early Rains	
7. Tishrei (Ethanim)	September–October	Plowing	**Festival of Tabernacle Rosh Hashanah***
8. Heshvan (Bul)	October–November	Sowing Wheat & Barley	
9. Kieslev	November–December	Winter Rains	**Hanukkah***
10. Tebeth	December–January	Almond Bloom	
11. Shebat	January–February	Citrus Harvest	
12. Adar	February–March	Frequent Rains	**Purim***
13. Adar Sheni	Intercalary Month		
Shabbat following the child's twelfth or thirteenth birthday			Ceremony of Bar / Bat Mitzvah*

*These Feasts are not commanded by God to the people of Israel
2. Counting the days (the Omer) is a command given by God to set the time leading to the next feast/ Pentecost

The civil calendar begins with the Jewish New Year at Rosh Hashanah (Tishrei–September/October). Our calendar is a solar calendar and found its beginnings with the decree of Pope Gregory XIII in 1582. This calendar is a reformed version of the Julian calendar. The Julian calendar came out of the Roman calendar and at the time was enforced by Julius Caesar. It is not clear where the idea for this calendar originated. Some speculations refer to it as an old version of the Egyptian calendar.

Rosh Chodesh "Head of the Month"

The Moon Seasons

He made the moon to mark the seasons. (Psalm 104:19)

Blow the trumpets in times of gladness, too, sounding them at your annual festivals and at the beginning of each month. And blow the trumpets over your burnt offerings and peace offerings. The trumpets will remind the Lord your God of his covenant with you. I am the Lord your God. (Numbers 10:10)

The common people will bow down and worship the Lord in front of this gateway on Sabbath days and the days of new moon celebrations. (Ezekiel 46:3)

Rosh Chodesh (translating to head of the month) is the name for the first day of every month in the Hebrew sacred calendar marked by the appearance of the new moon. Contrasted with the astronomical definition of new moon (which is not visible to the naked eye), the new moon in the Hebrew calendar is marked by the day and hour that the new crescent is observed. It is considered a minor holiday, meaning that it is not a Shabbat but it is very similar to one, being a day to gather for worship and to cease commercial activity. All other kinds of work were permitted, separating it from the Shabbat.

It was practice in the time of Gamaliel II (circa 100 AD) that two reliable eye witnesses would testify to the Sanhedrin of having seen the new lunar crescent at sunset. The news about Rosh Chodesh would then be communicated throughout Israel and the diaspora. This system was later discarded in favor of the fixed calendar developed by Hillel II (fourth century AD).

The entire Jewish calendar was dependent upon knowing when Rosh Chodesh began. Without this information, the set times for the festivals and holidays would be lost.

The Sanctification of the Month

Despite the existence of a fixed calendar, Rosh Chodesh is still announced in synagogues on the preceding Shabbat (called *Shabbat Mevarchim* or "The Shabbat of Blessing;" the new month) and an additional prayer is recited asking God to bless the coming month. If the Sabbath occurs exactly one day before the new moon, however, it is called *Shabbat Machar Chodesh* (Shabbat of tomorrow's moon) and Samuel 20:18–42 is read instead of the assigned weekly readings. If the Sabbath falls on the day of the new moon itself, it is called *Sabbath Rosh Chodesh* and an additional Torah reading (Numbers 28:9–15; Isaiah 66:1–24) is recited during services.

The following is an example of a traditional petition to the Lord for a good month that is recited at the end of the Shabbat Torah reading:

> *May it be Thy will, Lord, our God and God of our fathers, that You begin for us this month for good and for blessing. May You give to us long life, a life of peace, a life of goodness, a life of blessing, a life of sustenance, a life of physical health, a life in which there is fear of heaven and fear of sin, a life in which there is no shame or humiliation; a life of wealth and honor, a life in which we love Torah and fear God; a life in which the LORD fulfills the requests of our hearts for good. Amen. Selah.*

It is customary to announce the time at which the new moon will appear in Jerusalem. First the congregation recites:

> *The one who performed miracles for our forefathers and redeemed them from slavery to freedom, may He redeem us soon and gather in our exiles from the four corners of the earth; then all Israel shall be friends. Let us say: Amen.*

The cantor then announces the precise time of Rosh Chodesh in Jerusalem:

> *Rosh Chodesh (says name of the Hebrew month) will be on the day (says Hebrew day of the week) that comes to us and to all Israel for good.*

Sabbatical Year & Jubilee Year

The text from Leviticus 25 is a continuation of chapter 23, primarily dealing with the Hebrew festal calendar. Added now in Leviticus 25 are these two celebrations based on the Sabbath principle.

Every seventh year is a Sabbatical Year and no agricultural activities should be engaged. This practice is a benefit to the soil, but it is also a recognition that all produce belongs to God and that He bestows it freely on His people. The text in Leviticus 25:18–22 reveals an appeal to keep God's law, which will bring rich blessings. These blessings include security in the land against external threats. Furthermore, God promises to supply enough food during years of agricultural activity to cover periods in which the land lies fallow, such as during the sabbatical year.

The seventh year was also a time of instruction in the law of God for all the people of Israel:

> Then Moses gave them this command: "At the end of every seventh year, the Year of Release,

during the Festival of Shelters, you must read this Book of Instruction to all the people of Israel when they assemble before the Lord your God at the place he chooses. Call them all together—men, women, children, and the foreigners living in your towns—so they may hear this Book of Instruction and learn to fear the Lord your God and carefully obey all the terms of these instructions. Do this so that your children who have not known these instructions will hear them and will learn to fear the Lord your God. Do this as long as you live in the land you are crossing the Jordan to occupy." (Deuteronomy 31:10–13)

The Hebrew word for *jubilee* is related to a term that means "ram" or "ram's horn." The ram's horn is to be sounded throughout Israel on the Day of Atonement to announce the beginning of the fiftieth year, the Year of Jubilee.

In addition, you must count off seven Sabbath years, seven sets of seven years, adding up to forty–nine years in all. Then on the Day of Atonement in the fiftieth year, blow the ram's horn loud and long throughout the land. Set this year apart as holy, a time to proclaim freedom throughout the land for all who live there. It will be a jubilee year for you, when each of you may return to the land that belonged to your ancestors and return to your own clan. This fiftieth year will be a jubilee for you. During that year you must not plant your fields or store away any of the crops that grow on their own, and don't gather the grapes from your unpruned vines. It will be a jubilee year for you, and you must keep it holy. But you may eat whatever the land produces on its own. In the Year of Jubilee each

of you may return to the land that belonged to
your ancestors. (Leviticus 25:8–13)

Jubilee is a year of release and liberty. In that year, people
are to return to their land possession, i.e., their ancestral property. Captives were set free, slaves released, and debtors forgiven
(Leviticus 25:23–25, 39–55). It gave new opportunity to people
who had fallen on hard times. However, the Jubilee did not equal-
ize all possessions in Israel, since possessions such as cattle and
money were not reallocated. This law prohibits the amassing of
large estates, which would reduce many Israelites to tenant status
on their ancestral land (Isaiah 5:8).

In selling or purchasing property, the price was calculated
according to how many years have passed since the Jubilee. It was
not the estate itself that was to be sold or purchased, but rather the
number of years that crops could be harvested before the next jubilee
(Leviticus 25:15–16). Since all the Israelites eventually return to their
inherited land, the act of selling agricultural land essentially means
leasing (see exception Leviticus 25:29–31).

The Year of Jubilee is no longer observed. Some Jewish scholars
believe the Jubilee was regularly celebrated until the northern kingdom of Israel was exiled by the Assyrians. It is also believed that after
the destruction of the Second Temple and the disbandment of the
Sanhedrin (supreme rabbinical court), the Jubilee year was no longer
dated and recorded in any form.

The Jubilee presents a beautiful picture of the New Testament
themes of redemption and forgiveness. Christ is the redeemer who
came to set free those who are slaves and prisoners to sin (Romans
8:2; Galatians 5:1, 3:22). The debt of sin we owe to God was paid on
the cross as Jesus died on our behalf (Colossians 2:13–14). Our debt
is forever forgiven. We are no longer in bondage, no longer slaves
to sin. Freed by Christ, we can truly enter the rest God provides,
and cease laboring to make ourselves acceptable to God by our own
works (Hebrews 4:9–10).

The Commonwealth of Israel

Jesus identifies himself as a Jew in John 4:21. He clearly states "salvation is from the Jews." The messiah, Jesus Christ, came from the Jews and not from the Samaritans or (by implication) from the gentiles. He was not merely a human being but also fully God. In Romans 9:4, we learn that God adopted the Israelites. It lists six extraordinary privileges, blessings given only, yes, only to the Israelites—adoption, law, glory (probably refers to the glory of God in the tabernacle and temple), worship, covenants, and promises. The gentiles as a people were cut off from these privileges. We were without Christ, aliens, strangers, excluded from citizenship (the commonwealth) without hope and without God. In Ephesians, Paul reminds us that we Gentiles were called "uncircumcised heathens" by the Jews.

Christ brought peace and united Jews and Gentiles (believers in Christ) into one people, by giving His own body on the cross. He broke down the wall of hostility that separates them, by creating in Himself one new people from the two groups. Together as one body, Christ reconciled both groups to God by means of His death on the cross, and our hostility toward each other was put to death. Now all of us can come to the Father through the same Holy Spirit because of what Christ has done for us.

At this moment, I urge you to consider for a moment what you have received. Paul states in Romans 8 that God's saving promises have been fulfilled for the gentiles. Indeed, the

---

INSIGHT

The First Temple:

According to Jewish tradition, the temple was built at the same site on Mount Moriah where Abraham nearly sacrificed his son Isaac (2 Chronicles 3:1–3).

Second Temple Period:

This period spans from the rebuilding of the second temple after the Babylonian exile to the destruction by the Romans (roughly 515 BC to 70 AD). The sects of the Pharisees, Sadducees, Essenes, and Zealots were formed during this period.

Zealots:

The term *zealot* was frequently used for one that is zealous on behalf of God. Zealots were a political movement and sought to incite the people to rebel against the Roman Empire by expelling them from the Holy Land by force of arms (Jewish-Roman War, 66–70).

The Second Temple:

The structure dedicated in the time of Zerubbabel was but a pale shadow of Solomon's Temple (Ezra 3:12; Haggai 2:3). In time, however, it grew to eclipse in grandeur and splendor. Herod the Great began a tremendous renovation project (20-19 B.C.) that resulted in the second temple taking its place among the great wonders of the ancient world. During Jesus's ministry, the courtyards surrounding the temple were still under construction and were finished only a few short years before its destruction by the Romans in 70 AD.

church now enjoys the spiritual blessings promised to Israel: the gift of the spirit (8:9), adoption as God's children (8:14–17), future glory (8:17, 30), election (8:33), and the promise of never being severed from God's love (8:35–39). In Romans 9:25–26, Paul quotes Hosea 2:23 and 1:10 to illustrate the stunning grace of God—that those who are not my people "will be called 'sons of the living God.'"

You do not have to read and learn about the Feast of Israel simply in search for knowledge. In Christ, you can engage personally to celebrate the feasts by rejoicing in what Jesus, our Messiah, has done for you. You are a holy temple for the Lord.

So now you gentiles are no longer strangers and foreigners. You are citizens along with all of God's holy people. You are members of God's family. Together, we are his house, built on the foundation of the apostles and the prophets. And the cornerstone is Christ Jesus himself. We are carefully joined together in him, becoming a holy temple for the Lord. Through him you gentiles are also being made part of this dwelling where God lives by his Spirit (Ephesians 2:19–22, NLT).

Man-Made Laws

Studying the Feasts of Israel requires distinguishing between God's commands, Jewish traditions, and "man-made laws." Recognizing these differences will profoundly open our understanding of the Feasts. Let us have a look into the religious situation and understanding of the Jewish faith during the second temple period which includes the time of Jesus Christ here on Earth.

A) What Did God Command?

We find in the Bible clear and specific instructions about the feasts. For example:

> Obey these instructions as a lasting ordinance for you (the people of Israel) and your descendants. When you enter the land that the

Lord will give you as he promised, observe this ceremony. And when your children ask you, "What does this ceremony mean to you?" then tell them, "It is the Passover sacrifice to the Lord…" (Exodus 12:24–27)

B) What Are Traditions?

You can tell a story in many ways. Many Jewish traditions began just from how a specific story was told. We will concentrate only on these traditions that provide a greater understanding of Jesus Christ and our faith in Him. You will find helpful guidance on how to celebrate these traditions in your home, the goal being to bring Jesus Christ into the center of your celebration.

C) What Are Man-Made Laws?

In the course of time, in particular by the second temple period, a strong emphasis on man-made laws had developed. To understand this better, we will now zoom in on several Jewish religious groups which were active at the time of Christ, such as the Pharisees, Sadducees and the Essenes. Each of these groups left their mark on our Christian faith today through their teachings and preservation of literature. They all awaited the Messiah, a leader anointed by God and direct descendant of David, who would reunite the Jewish tribes and, perhaps, rule them as King of Israel.

The Pharisees

The inevitable question of the Jews in the exilic community was, why did God punish us in this way? The answer was not hard to find. They had violated the Sinai Covenant, and the Lord had requited them for disloyalty (Nehemiah 1:5–

The Pharisees

11; Daniel 9:4–19). Recognizing this, the religious leaders in exile began to rectify the situation. If Israel was ever again to experience God's favor nationally, there had to be a vigorous effort to observe all the covenant requirements. This raised a serious problem. Many of the requirements were addressed to a people living an agrarian life in the land of Canaan. How could the Jews in exile keep these regulations?

In a historic move, the Jewish scholars set about adapting and amplifying the 613 commandments found in the Pentateuch. Since the aim was to achieve as much compliance as humanly possible, these scholars sought to make it difficult to break the law. This they did by "hedging the Law" or gradually devising other commandments to surround and protect the original ones. These new rulings were not written down but taught orally. They became known as the "Oral Torah" or the "tradition of the elders or fathers" (Matthew 15:2; Galatians 1:14).

We find Jesus speaking about these traditions in Mark:

> So the Pharisees and teachers of religious law asked him, "Why don't your disciples follow our age–old tradition? They eat without first performing the hand–washing ceremony." Jesus replied, "You hypocrites! Isaiah was right when he prophesied about you, for he wrote, 'These people honor me with their lips, but their hearts are far from me. Their worship is a farce, for they teach man–made ideas as commands from God.' For you ignore God's law and substitute your own tradition." Then he said, "You skillfully sidestep God's law in order to hold on to your own tradition. For instance, Moses gave you this law from God:

INSIGHT

The word *Pentateuch* comes from the combination of the Greek "penta" and "teuchos" which can be translated "five" and "scroll." It refers to the first five books of the Bible: Genesis, Exodus, Leviticus, Numbers, and Deuteronomy.

These five books are also known as the Torah, which is the Hebrew word meaning "Law."

'Honor your father and mother,' and 'Anyone who speaks disrespectfully of father or mother must be put to death. 'But you say it is all right for people to say to their parents, 'Sorry, I can't help you. For I have vowed to give to God what I would have given to you. 'In this way, you let them disregard their needy parents. And so you cancel the word of God in order to hand down your own tradition. And this is only one example among many others." (Mark 7:5–13)

Over time, the Oral Torah acquired legitimacy by being ascribed to Moses himself. The tradition arose that on Mount Sinai, two Torahs were delivered to Moses: the Written Torah and the Oral Torah. Both were equally authoritative. This concept of the dual Torah became the hallmark of Pharisaism and is still fundamental for Orthodox Judaism. Eventually much of this legal material was written down in what is called the *Mishnah*. This body of literature was commented on and expanded over several centuries and eventually codified in the *Talmud*. For Orthodox or traditional Jews today, the *Talmud* (meaning instruction, learning) constitutes the basis for their religion.

The Sadducees

The Sadducees were a party of Jews that were active in Judea during the Second Temple period. None of the writings of the Sadducees have survived, so the little we know about them comes from their Pharisaic opponents and the Bible.

The Sadducees

During the time of the New Testament era, the Sadducees were known to be wealthy aristocrats of the high-priestly families of Jerusalem. The Sadducees' main focus was on the rituals associated with the temple worship, and they generally collaborated with the Roman rulers. Because they were accommodating to Rome and were the wealthy upper class, they did not relate well to the common man, nor did the common man hold them in high regards.

The Sadducees were liberal in their willingness to incorporate Hellenism into their lives, something the Pharisees opposed. The Sadducees rejected the idea of the Oral Law observed by the Pharisees and accepted only a literal interpretation of the Pentateuch as authoritative. They were the anti-super naturalists of Christ's day, denying the truth of bodily resurrection, of future punishment and reward, and of the existence of angels (Acts 23:8). Pharisees and Sadducees had little in common.

Pharisees were:

- ritualists
- legalists
- separatists

Sadducees were:

- rationalists
- liberals
- compromisers & political opportunists

However, both groups united in their opposition of Christ (Matthew 22:23–33). John the Baptist publicly addressed them as deadly snakes (Matthew 3:7).

The Essenes

The Dead Sea Scrolls are a treasure to any theologian or Bible translator, but in particular to the Jewish people and nation. Who were these people that wrote them? They are believed to be the literary remains of a Jewish sect—generally identified as the Essenes—who during the period of about 150 BC to 68 AD occupied a site along the northwestern shore of the Dead Sea.

Qumran Caves

Presenting over the community was a council consisting of twelve laymen representing the biblical ideal of the twelve tribes of Israel and three priests. The group clearly disapproved of the corrupted rituals at the Jerusalem temple and viewed itself as the true priesthood (1QS 9:3–5).

These "Sons of Zadok" (Zadokite priestly family from the Jerusalem high priesthood) were the undisputed authorities for the sectarians. These priests came to be the undisputed leaders of the community. After about twenty years, a "teacher of righteousness" arose to lead the movement. He was himself a priest, in all likelihood a Zadokite. The interpretations of the "teacher" were considered infallible inasmuch as God directly revealed hidden truth to him. After his death, an official called the "overseer" carried on his role.

INSIGHT

1QS stands for Cave 1 / Qumran / *Serekah*, meaning rule. It contains the Rule of the Community, also called the Manual of Discipline. Scroll size: six and a half feet long and ten inches wide.

QH contains the Thanksgiving Hymns. They are similar in style to canonical Psalms. This scroll also gives insight into the ethos and mindset of the Qumran community. Scroll size: ten feet long and about twelve inches wide.

Qumran Excavation and
Suggested Reconstruction

The Qumran community strictly lived by the sacred calendar by observing the feasts and rituals at their divinely ordained times. Their theology was marked by legalism, i.e., they believed in salvation by works. A yearly review of all members was held regarding their performance and conduct. There was very little room for confession and repentance at Qumran. Only if the sins were inadvertent could one be restored, and even then, the restoration involved a virtual repeat of a probationary admission. If one compares the Halakah of Qumran to that of the Pharisees pictured in the New Testament and later in the *Mishnah*, it is generally more strict and extends the application of the various rulings.

As a "holy house for Aaron" they awaited the coming of "the prophet and the messiahs of Aaron and Israel" (1QS 9:11). In essence, they believed in two messiahs:

- a priest (from the line of Aaron)
- a king (from the line of King David)

The New Testament combines the functions of both the high priest and the Davidic king in the person of Jesus Christ (Matthew 1:1; Hebrew 4:14). However, they were convinced that the last days had begun and the final intervention of God and his messiahs was imminent.

The teacher of righteousness believed that God was the blessed controller of all things and foreordained all things that transpire in the world. The sovereignty of God is a keynote throughout the thanksgiving hymns found at Qumran.

> By Your wisdom, You have established the successive generations and before You created them You knew all their works for ever and ever. For apart from You nothing is done, and without Your will nothing is known. You have formed every spirit and You determined their deeds and judgment for all their works (1QH 9:7–9).

How does one experience forgiveness and cleansing? The teacher, like the New Testament writers, located the source of cleansing in the prevenient grace of God. There are several passages that make this clear.

Example:

> But all the children of Your truth You bring before You in forgiveness, cleansing them from their rebellious acts in the multiplicity of Your goodness, and by the abundance of Your compassion maintaining them before You for ever and ever (1QH 15:29b–31a).

Though both stressed the priority of grace, for the teacher, "works of the law" were essential for obtaining final salvation. For the New Testament, "works of the law" result in condemnation (Galatians 2:16, 3:10–14). Instead, one needs to be liberated from the "works of the law" and united with Jesus Christ in his death, burial, and resurrection (Romans 6:1–4). Paradoxically, this results in a true fulfillment of the law (Romans 8:1–8). Union with Christ brings about justification and sanctification (Romans 8:1–8). As a result, the love of God floods the believer's life and issues in a lifestyle exceeding all the law's demands—this is the new "law of Christ" (1 Corinthians 9:21; Galatians 5:13–25).

Paul's critique of his non-believing fellow Jews states:

> Israel, who did strive for the righteousness that is based on the law, did not succeed in fulfilling that law. Why not? Because they did not strive for it on the basis of faith, but as if it were based on works. They have stumbled over the stumbling stone, as it is written, "See, I am laying in Zion a stone that will make people stumble, a rock that will make them fall, and whoever believes in him will not be put to shame." (Romans 9:31–33)

We can be quite sure that legalism was a real danger, not only at Qumran but also among the Pharisees. Interestingly enough, Jesus sided with the Sadducees on one point, namely that the written Torah alone possessed binding authority for faith and practice.

Text: Matthew 5:17–20, 15:2–9; Mark 7:8–13

A number of scholars have suggested that at least several of Jesus's sayings and parables may well have had the Essenes as the intended foil. Perhaps the clearest instance occurs in the Sermon on the Mount.

> You have heard that is was said, You shall love your neighbor and hate your enemy. (Matthew 5:43)

The first part of the citation is, of course, found in the Hebrew Bible (Leviticus 19:18; Deuteronomy 10:19), but nowhere in Jewish sources do we find an exhortation to hate one's enemies, except in the sectarian literature stemming from Qumran (1QS 1:4, 9–10). He may have been deliberately contrasting his behavioral standard for disciples with that of the Essenes.

Charts

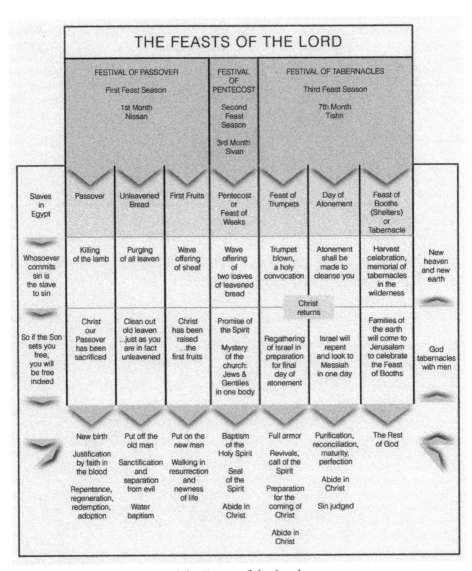

The Feasts of the Lord

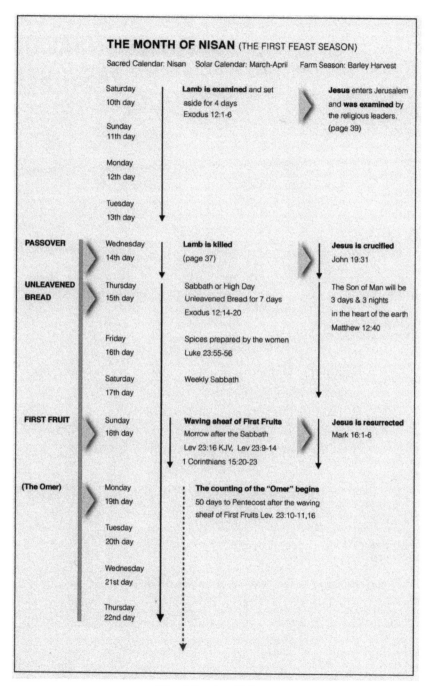

THE MONTH OF NISAN (THE FIRST FEAST SEASON)

Sacred Calendar: Nisan   Solar Calendar: March-April   Farm Season: Barley Harvest

	Saturday 10th day	**Lamb is examined** and set aside for 4 days Exodus 12:1-6	**Jesus** enters Jerusalem and **was examined** by the religious leaders. (page 39)
	Sunday 11th day		
	Monday 12th day		
	Tuesday 13th day		
PASSOVER	Wednesday 14th day	**Lamb is killed** (page 37)	**Jesus is crucified** John 19:31
UNLEAVENED BREAD	Thursday 15th day	Sabbath or High Day Unleavened Bread for 7 days Exodus 12:14-20	The Son of Man will be 3 days & 3 nights in the heart of the earth Matthew 12:40
	Friday 16th day	Spices prepared by the women Luke 23:55-56	
	Saturday 17th day	Weekly Sabbath	
FIRST FRUIT	Sunday 18th day	**Waving sheaf of First Fruits** Morrow after the Sabbath Lev 23:16 KJV, Lev 23:9-14 1 Corinthians 15:20-23	**Jesus is resurrected** Mark 16:1-6
(The Omer)	Monday 19th day	**The counting of the "Omer" begins** 50 days to Pentecost after the waving sheaf of First Fruits Lev. 23:10-11,16	
	Tuesday 20th day		
	Wednesday 21st day		
	Thursday 22nd day		

The Month of Nisan

CHAPTER 3

THE FESTIVAL OF PASSOVER

THE FIRST FEAST SEASON

Overview

The Festival of Passover combines a group of three feasts. It is the beginning of the First Feast Season commanded by the Lord.

The Feast of Passover:

- Killing the lamb and placing its blood on the doorpost
- First month (Nisan), fourteenth day
- Christ our Passover has been sacrificed
- You are no longer slaves to sin
- So if the Son sets you free, you will be free indeed

    Text: Exodus 12:1–13; Leviticus 23:5; 1 Corinthians 5:7; Romans 6:6, 16–18,22; John 8:34

The Feast of Unleavened Bread:

- Purging of all leaven (symbol of sin) on the first month, fifteenth day, for seven days (the first and seventh day are Sabbath days)
- Clean out old leaven, just as you are in fact unleavened

    Text: Leviticus 23:6–8; 1 Corinthians 5:7,8

The Feast of First Fruit:

- Wave offering of sheaf (promise of harvest to come)
  Day after Sabbath (It is a Sabbath)

- Christ has been raised: the First Fruit

  Text: Leviticus 23:9–14; 1 Corinthians 15:20–23

The Feast of Passover

Text: Exodus 12:1–14, 12:46, 21–29; Leviticus 23:4–5;
Numbers 33:3; Deuteronomy 16:1–8; Psalm 113–118

The Feast of Passover marks the beginning of the first of three feast seasons and is a memorial celebration of God's deliverance from Egypt. Only a circumcised person was allowed to eat of it that was part of Abraham's covenant with God.

On Passover, the male head of every family had to kill a one-year-old lamb without spot or blemish and offer it as a sacrifice to God. This lamb needed to be kept aside and inspected from the tenth to the fourteenth day of the month of Nisan. The lamb was killed on the doorstep of the house on the evening of the fourteenth day. The blood was then sprinkled on the doorframe (doorposts and lintel).

After the temple in Jerusalem was built, the Jews brought the lamb there to kill it. The celebrating and worshiping Jews would be led by the Levites in singing out of the Psalms, typically from Psalms 113–118. Today these Psalms are known as the *Hallel* and are traditionally sung at the end of the Passover meal. The lamb had to be eaten roasted with bitter herbs and unleavened bread, without breaking any bones. All leaven was removed from

One–Year–Old Lamb
Without Spot Or Blemish

the house. For seven days, beginning with the night of the Passover, the Jews ate bread without leaven.

Each Jewish family had to eat the Passover meal in haste, their loins girded in preparation to leave Egypt. Nothing could be left over from the lamb the next day. At midnight, the angel of the Lord would pass over every house on which the sprinkled blood of the lamb was found. The angel would spare the life of the first born son of that house.

Passover Today

Since the destruction of the temple, the Jews are no longer able to sacrifice the Passover lamb at the temple. However, the Feast of Passover is still a very special festival for the Jews. It begins with the day before Passover. Often the son helps the father with the mitzvah (a meritorious deed). Bread pieces are laid about in the house, symbolizing the leaven. In this meritorious deed, the father leads the ritual of cleansing the house before he proclaims it clean. Only then is the house ready for the *matzo* (unleavened bread).

After the father returns from the synagogue on Passover, the family gathers around the table to begin the Seder ceremony. A narration called *Haggadah* (Hebrew for "telling") from Exodus tells the story about Passover. Faithfully the Jews tell the story and teach their children to remember how God freed them out of Egypt. One chair at the table is set with a cup of wine for Elijah. The Jews believed that he would come on this day (in the person of John the Baptist) to announce the coming of the Messiah.

Text: Exodus 12:15–20,34,39

Matzo bread, a prepared lamb shank in place of the lamb, and bitter herbs, symbolic of the bitterness of slavery, are found on the table to celebrate Passover. The Jews added other symbols like red wine being symbolic of the blood of the lamb. A mixture of apples and nuts tells of the bricks they had to make. Parsley dipped in salt water tells how God brought them through the Red Sea. Three loaves of matzo, each wrapped in a napkin, represent Abraham, Isaac, and Jacob.

For the Messianic Jews, the three loaves represent the Trinity. In the beginning of the ceremony, the middle loaf is broken in two. One of these pieces is then hidden behind a pillow until the end of the Haggadah. The broken unleavened piece of bread is symbolic of Jesus's death. The hiding of the matzo shows his burial, and the finding of the matzo shows the resurrection of Jesus Christ.

Passover is the very feast Jesus celebrated with his disciples before his crucifixion. It was during this feast that he washed the feet of the disciples and celebrated with them the Lord's supper.

Text: Luke 22:19; 1 Corinthians 11:24 (KJV); Isaiah 53

Passover and Jesus Christ

Text: Exodus 4:22–23; Luke 19:37; Matthew 22:15–24; 1 Corinthians 5:7; Hebrew 12:22–24

Jesus Christ is our Passover lamb that was sacrificed and died for our sins. Christ crucified fulfilled the Feast of Passover. Equally to the lamb, Jesus was examined, but by the religious leaders of Israel.

- Pilate, who pronounced that he could find no fault in Him. John 18:28,38, 19:4–6; Matthew 27:1–25
- Herod. Luke 23:8–12
- Caiaphas. John 11:49–53, 18:13–14, 19–24,28
- The centurion. Matthew 27:54
- The thief on the cross. Luke 23:39–43

Just like by the Passover lamb, Jesus was crucified on the fourteenth day and neither were any bones broken in His body. Jesus was taken down from the cross before sundown. He did not remain on the cross to the next day, just as there was nothing left over the next day of the Passover lamb. The Israelites were safe in their houses because of the sacrificed blood of the lamb on their doorframe. Jesus

Christ is the Lamb of God, our Passover lamb that was sacrificed for our sins. It is because of the shed blood of our Lord on the cross that the sins are forgiven of those who put their trust and faith in him. Jesus died for our sins. We are justified in the eyes of God. It is written:

> Therefore, since we have been made right
> in God's sight by faith, we have peace with God
> because of what Jesus Christ our Lord has done
> for us. (Romans 5:1)

We are free indeed and no longer slaves to sin (Romans 6:6,16–18,22; John 8:34). Your faith in Jesus Christ will bring you new hope and joy.

The Lord's Passover Meal

I pray that God, the source of hope, will fill you completely with joy and peace because you trust in him. Then you will overflow with confident hope through the power of the Holy Spirit. (Romans 15:13)

Jesus ended the Passover meal by leading the disciples to the communion table.

> As they were eating, Jesus took some bread and blessed it. Then he broke it in pieces and gave it to the disciples, saying, "Take this and eat it, for this is my body." And he took a cup of wine

and gave thanks to God for it. He gave it to them and said, "Each of you drink from it, for this is my blood, which confirms the covenant between God and his people. It is poured out as a sacrifice to forgive the sins of many. (Matthew 26:26–28)

Circumcision was the sign and seal of the blessings and promises of the old covenant. Only the circumcised were entitled to partake of Passover. A person under the new covenant relationship with Jesus Christ has the privilege to partake of the Lord's table. This person is not circumcised by the flesh but of the heart by the Holy Spirit. To him belong the blessings and promises of the new covenant. To him belongs the awaited priceless inheritance in heaven.

When you came to Christ, you were "circumcised," but not by a physical procedure. Christ performed a spiritual circumcision—the cutting away of your sinful nature. For you were buried with Christ when you were baptized. And with him you were raised to new life because you trusted the mighty power of God who raised Christ from the dead. You were dead because of your sins and because your sinful nature was not yet cut away. Then God made you alive with Christ, for he forgave all our sins. He canceled the record of the charges against us and took it away by nailing it to the cross. In this way, he disarmed the spiritual rulers and authorities. He shamed them publicly by his victory over them on the cross (Colossians 2:11–15).

Text: Galatians 3:26, 6:15; John 3:1–7; Philippians 3:3; Romans 2:28,29

The Doctrine of Atonement and Justification

God the Father made Christ to be regarded and treated as "sin" even though Christ himself never sinned (Hebrew 4:15; Galatians 3:13). God did this for our sake. God regarded and treated "our" sin (the sin of all who would believe in Christ) as if our sin belonged not to us but to Christ himself. Thus Christ "died for all" (2 Corinthians 5:14) and, as Peter wrote, "He himself bore our sins in His body on the tree" (1 Peter 2:24). In becoming sin "for our sake," Christ became our substitute—that is, Christ took our sin upon himself and bore the wrath of God (the punishment that we deserve) in our place ("for our sake"). Thus, the foundational doctrine of the Christian faith is the substitutionary atonement that Christ has provided the atoning sacrifice as "our" substitute for the sins of all who believe (Romans 3:23–25).

Christ's Crucifixion

Isaiah prophesied specifically regarding the coming Savior (the suffering servant). "Surely He has born our griefs" (Isaiah 53:4); "He was crushed for our iniquities" (Isaiah 53:5); "He shall bear their iniquities" (Isaiah 53:11); "He bore the sin of many" (Isaiah 53:12).

In a precise fulfillment of this prophecy, Christ became "sin" for those who believe in Him, so that in him we might become the righteousness of God. This means that just as God imputed our sin and guilt to Christ ("He made Him to be sin"), so God also imputes the righteousness of Christ—a righteousness that is not our own—to all who believe in Christ.

Because Christ bore the sins of those who believe, God regards and treats believers as having the legal status of "righteous." This righteousness belongs to believers because they are "in Him," that is, "in Christ" (Romans 3:22, 5:18; 1 Corinthians 1:30). Therefore, "the righteousness of God (which is imputed to believers)" is also the righteousness of Christ—; that is, the righteousness and the legal status that belongs to Christ as a result of Christ having lived as one who "knew no sin." This then is the heart of the doctrine of justification: God regards (or counts) believers as forgiven and God declares and treats them as forgiven, because God the Father has imputed the believer's sin to Christ and because God the Father likewise imputes Christ's righteousness to the believer (Romans 4:6–8, 5:18, 10:3, 10:6–8).

Isaiah 53:11, "the righteous one, my servant, shall make many to be accounted righteous."

The Sprinkling of Blood

We can find three events in the Old Testament where blood was sprinkled upon people:

1) At the establishment of the Old Covenant:

> For after Moses had read each of God's commandments to all the people, he took the blood of calves and goats, along with water, and sprinkled both the book of God's law and all the people, using hyssop branches and scarlet wool. (Hebrews 9:19) (See also text: Exodus 24:5–8)

2) At the priestly anointing of Aaron and his sons:

> Next Moses took some of the anointing oil and some of the blood that was on the altar, and he sprinkled them on Aaron and his garments and on his sons and their garments. In this way, he made Aaron and his sons and their garments holy. (Leviticus 8:30)

3) At the purification for a cleansed leper:

> As for the live bird, he shall take it together with the cedar wood and the scarlet string and the hyssop, and shall dip them and the live bird in the blood of the bird that was slain over the running water. He shall then sprinkle seven times the one who is to be cleansed from the leprosy and shall pronounce him clean, and shall let the live bird go free over the open field. (Leviticus 14:6–7)

In the New Testament, we find also the sprinkling of blood, the shed blood of Jesus Christ on the cross. Meditate upon the given scripture texts in view of the Old Testament.

1) We are now under the New Covenant.
2) We are ordained as priests to Him.
3) We are cleansed from our corruption and sin.

> You have come to Jesus, the one who mediates the New Covenant between God and people, and to the sprinkled blood, which speaks of forgiveness instead of crying out for vengeance like the blood of Abel. (Hebrews 12:24)

> According to the foreknowledge of God the Father, by the sanctifying work of the Spirit, to obey Jesus Christ and be sprinkled with His blood: May grace and peace be yours in the fullest measure. (1 Peter 1:2)

> But you are not like that, for you are a chosen people. You are royal priests, a holy nation, God's very own possession. As a result, you can show others the goodness of God, for he called you out of the darkness into his wonderful light. (1 Peter 2:9)

> He has made us a Kingdom of priests for God his Father. All glory and power to him forever and ever! Amen. (Revelation 1:6)

> Let us go right into the presence of God with sincere hearts fully trusting him. For our guilty consciences have been sprinkled with Christ's blood to make us clean, and our bodies have been washed with pure water. (Hebrews 10:22)

Time with God

Take some time with God to reflect on what you've learned. What has God already revealed to you? Write down whatever God speaks to your heart, along with any insights you might have.

Every so often, you will find additional Bible verses, questions, or songs. Find a quiet place and expect God to reveal himself to you while you work through this section(s) of "Time With God." You may want to use the songs to express your heart in prayer to God. Know that He likes to hear your voice.

Jesus found Himself praying alone to His father in the garden of Gethsemane. This happened right after a wonderful time celebrating Passover in Jerusalem with many of His close friends. Have you ever found yourself alone speaking to God? Perhaps it was during a time in which you knew He was the only one who could understand you. Was He your only hope? Jesus Christ is the Passover Lamb. By His death on the cross, He made atonement for my and your sins—even for sins that we think are too big to ever be forgiven. I am reconciled with God and nothing shall separate me anymore from His love.

Have You Had a Gethsemane?
By William J. Gaither

In the garden He went to pray
when it seemed hope was gone.
He prayed with a broken heart.
He prayed all alone.
Have you had a Gethsemane?
Have you prayed in despair?
In the dark of those weary hours
did the Lord meet you there?
Have you had a Gethsemane?
Have you prayed the night through?
Have you shed tears of agony
when no hope was in view?
Have you prayed, "If it be Thy will

may this cup pass from me?
But if it's Thy will, dear Lord,
I will bear it for thee?"

We are more than conquerors through Him who loved us:

> What, then, shall we say in response to these things? If God is for us, who can be against us? He who did not spare his own Son, but gave him up for us all—how will he not also, along with him, graciously give us all things? Who will bring any charge against those whom God has chosen? It is God who justifies. Who then is the one who condemns? No one. Christ Jesus who died – more than that, who was raised to life – is at the right hand of God and is also interceding for us. Who shall separate us from the love of Christ? Shall trouble or hardship or persecution or famine or nakedness or danger or sword? As it is written: "For your sake we face death all day long; we are considered as sheep to be slaughtered." No, in all these things we are more than conquerors through him who loved us. For I am convinced that neither death nor life, neither angels nor demons, neither the present nor the future, nor any powers, neither height nor depth, nor anything else in all creation, will be able to separate us from the love of God that is in Christ Jesus our Lord. (Romans 8:31–39)

God's Plan for Salvation

All have sinned and fall short of the glory of God, being justified freely by His grace through the redemption that is in Christ Jesus. (Romans 3:23–24)

God demonstrates His own love toward us, in that while we were still sinners, Christ died for us. (Romans 5:8)

The wages of sin is death, but the gift of God is eternal life in Christ Jesus our Lord. (Romans 6:23)

But what does it say? "The word is near you, in your mouth and in your heart" (*that is, the word of faith which we preach*): that if you confess with your mouth the Lord Jesus and believe in your heart that God had raised Him from the dead, you will be saved. For with the heart one believes unto righteousness, and with the mouth confession is made unto salvation. (Romans 10:8–10)

Christ died for our sins according to the Scriptures, and that He was buried, and that He rose again on the third day according to the Scriptures. (1 Corinthians 15:4)

For God so loved the world that He gave His only begotten son, that whoever believes in Him should not perish but have everlasting life. For God did not send His Son into the world to condemn the world, but that the world through Him might be saved. (John 3:16–17)

By grace you have been saved through faith, and that not of yourselves; it is the gift of God, not of works, lest anyone should boast. (Ephesian 2:8–9)

Behold, I stand at the door and knock. If anyone hears My voice and opens the door, I will come in to him and dine with him, and he with Me. (Revelations 3:20)

This is the testimony: that God had given us eternal life, and this life is in His Son. He who had the Son has life; he who does not have the Son of God does not have life. These things I have written to you who believe in the name of the Son of God, that you may know that you have eternal life, and that you may continue to believe in the name of the Son of God. (1 John 5:11–13)

No Longer Slaves
Brian Johnson (Bethel), Jonathan D. Helser, Joel Case

Verse 1
You unravel me with a melody
You surround me with a song
Of deliverance from my enemies
Til all my fears are gone

Chorus
I'm no longer a slave to fear
I am a child of God
I'm no longer a slave to fear
I am a child of God

Verse 2
From my mother's womb, You have chosen me
Your love has called my name
I've been born again into Your family
Your blood flows through my veins

Chorus
I'm no longer a slave to fear
I am a child of God
I'm no longer a slave to fear
I am a child of God

Bridge
You split the sea so I could walk right through it
My fears were drowned in perfect love
You rescued me so I can stand and sing
I am a child of God
There's power in the name of Jesus
(You split the sea so I could walk right through it)
There's power in the name of Jesus
(My fears were drowned in perfect love)
There's power in the name of Jesus
(You rescued me so I can stand and sing)
To break every chain, to break every chain
To break every chain
(I am a child of God)
To break every chain, to break every chain
To break every chain
He breaks every chain, He breaks every chain
He breaks every chain
We're no longer slaves, we're no longer slaves
We're no longer slaves
He broke every chain
We're no longer slaves We're children of God

Chorus
You split the sea so I could walk right through it
My fears were drowned in perfect love
(perfect love)
You rescued me so I can stand and sing
I am a child of God
(hallelujah, hallelujah, hallelujah, hallelujah)
I am a child of God
(hallelu–hallelu–hallelujah)
(We're no longer slaves!)
I am a child of God

The Feast of Unleavened Bread

INSIGHT

Matzo (*Matza* or *Matzah*) is unleavened bread. Today, you can typically find matzo in two forms. A hard cracker-like one and a soft one which looks like Greek *pinta*. Traditionally, the flour has to be made from one of the five grains mentions in the Torah: wheat, barley, spelt, rye, or oats.

Unleavened
Bread

Text: Exodus 12:15–19, 23:14–15; Leviticus 23:6–8; Matthew 26:17–19; Luke 22:1–2

The very next day after Passover, the Feast of Unleavened Bread was held for seven days. No yeast was to be found for those seven days in their homes. For seven days, they had to eat unleavened bread. The feast was celebrated annually and marked the anniversary of Israel's leaving Egypt. Leaven symbolized the Israelites old life of slavery in Egypt that they left behind.

God was calling the people of Israel to faithfulness in celebrating the Feast of Unleavened Bread (Exodus 13:3–16) and consecrating all their firstborn in Israel, whether animal or human (Exodus 13:2). Every firstborn was regarded as belonging to the Lord. This feast reminds Israel that when the Egyptian firstborn died in the tenth plague, the Israelites were spared. *Consecrate* means "make holy by giving to God." Thus the firstborn of sacrificial animals, such as sheep and cattle, had to be sacrificed.

However, firstborn donkeys and humans had to be redeemed: a lamb was offered in sacrifice instead of them. Like at the Passover (Exodus 12:26–27) and now in the same way at the Feast of Unleavened Bread (Exodus 13:8–9), parents were to be faithful in both the doing and the telling of consecration: And when in time to come your son asks you, "What does this mean?" you shall say:

> Unleavened bread shall be eaten for seven days; no leavened bread shall be seen with you, and no leaven shall be seen with you in all your territory. You shall tell your son on that day, "It is because of what the LORD did for me when I came out of Egypt." And it shall be to you as a sign on your hand and as a memorial between your eyes, that the law of the LORD may be in your mouth. For with a strong hand the LORD has brought you out of Egypt. You shall therefore keep this statute at its appointed time from year to year. (Exodus 13:7–10)

The Lord's statutes were to be normative and governing for life in Israel.

> "Hear, O Israel! The Lord is our God, the Lord is one! You shall love the Lord your God with all your heart and with all your soul and with all your might. These words, which I am commanding you today, shall be on your heart. You shall teach them diligently to your sons and shall talk of them when you sit in your house and when you walk by the way and when you lie down and when you rise up. You shall bind them as a sign on your hand and they shall be as frontals on your forehead. You shall write them

on the doorposts of your house and on your
gates." (Deuteronomy 6:4–9)

Oh, the joys of those who do not follow
the advice of the wicked, or stand around with
sinners, or join in with mockers. But they delight
in the law of the Lord, meditating on it day and
night (Psalm 1:1–3).

The Symbol of Leaven

Leaven is often used as a picture for sin in the Bible. Jesus Christ
was the bread of life from heaven that had no sin (leaven), and as
such, He fulfilled the Feast of Unleavened Bread. Christ had never
sinned, yet He paid the penalty for our sin. Christ was the offering
so that we could be made right through Him with God. Jesus said in
His own words, John 6:35, "I am the bread of life. He who comes to
me shall never hunger, and he who believes in me shall never thirst."

Jesus Christ and the Feast of Unleavened Bread

For Christians, the Feast of Unleavened Bread shows us the second step in our walk with God. It teaches us to put off the old man
by appropriating the finished work of Jesus Christ. For the Jews,
Egypt represents the worldly system of sin and evil. God separated
and delivered the Jews out of Egypt. Likewise, we too ought to live
a holy life set apart and different from the world. The power of sin
has been broken. God's transforming work in us enables us to think
and live an acceptable sanctified life according to His will and for His
honor and glory.

Text: Galatians 5; Thessalonians 2:13, 4:3–4; 1 Peter
1:2; Philippians 2:12–13

The Feast of First Fruits

Text: Leviticus 23:9–16; 1 Corinthians 15:20–23; Joshua 5:10–21

Festive Decorated Sheaves of Grain

The Feast of First Fruits was held after the regular Sabbath day during the Feast of Unleavened Bread (Sunday). God ordered the Israelites to bring sheaves of the harvest first fruits to the priest. The priest would take the barley sheaves (first fruits) and wave them before the Lord in the temple on their behalf. Then come a series of sacrifices that would include a whole burnt offering, a grain offering, and a drink offering (reflecting the grape harvest). These acts are to dedicate and celebrate the entire harvest as a blessing from God given to His people. The Feast of First Fruits could not be celebrated when the Israelites wandered in the wilderness. They had no crops (harvest), of course. God provided for them the manna from heaven. They would celebrate the Feast after they entered the Promised Land.

Jesus Christ and the Feast of First Fruits

The term "first fruits" refers to a first sample of an agricultural crop that indicates the nature and quality of the rest of the crop. Therefore, Christ's resurrection body gives a foretaste of what those of believers will be like. Jesus fulfilled the Feast of First Fruits when he was resurrected as the first fruits from the dead.

We learn from the Bible that the time of Jesus's resurrection was "the close of the Sabbath." Jesus presented himself to God as the first fruits from the dead on Sunday—on the Feast of First Fruits. It was the same day the barley sheaf (first fruits) was waved before the Lord in the temple. God accepted Jesus as the first fruits wave offering from the dead. Therefore, the harvest—we—are accepted. All who believe in Jesus Christ as their personal savior represents this harvest. They will rise from the dead to eternal life.

The Feast of First Fruits in the Lives of Christians

In the previous feast, we throw off our old and sinful way of life. The Feast of First Fruits calls us to put on the new man that is truly righteous and holy, created after the likeness of God. We are allowing the Holy Spirit to renew our thoughts and attitudes. We allow him to live the resurrected life of Jesus Christ through us. In doing so, we enjoy the experience of what it means to have the peace of God. The Feast of Unleavened Bread and First Fruits represents the transforming work of God known as sanctification.

Text: Ephesians 4:24; 2 Corinthians 5:17; Romans 6:11–14; Galatians 5:16, 5:22–23; Colossians 3:15

Time with God

Did you ever think about the crucifixion from God's perspective? Imagine looking down from heaven and seeing Jerusalem and its people busily preparing the Feast of Passover. Imagine watching your son being mocked, beaten, and led outside of the city. He saw His Son (the Lamb of God) suffering and crucifixion on a hill called Golgotha. What must have been on God's heart? Talk with God about it. Read the following Bible verses. Write down what God reveals to you.

For He made Him who knew no sin to be sin for us, that we might become the righteousness of God in Him. (2 Corinthians 5:21)

Who committed no sin, Nor was deceit found in His mouth; who, when He was reviled, did not revile in return; when He suffered, He did not threaten, but committed Himself to Him who judges righteously; who Himself bore our sins in His own body on the tree, that we, having died to sin, might live for righteousness—by those stripes you were healed. (1 Peter 2:22–24)

Love Lifted Me

by Howard E. Smith, James Rowe, Michael T. Smith

I was sinking deep in sin, far from the peaceful shore.
Very deeply stained within, sinking to rise no more;
But the Master of the sea heard my despairing cry,
From the waters lifted me, now safe am I.
Love lifted me (even me)!
Love lifted me (even me)!
When nothing else could help,
Love lifted me!
All my heart to Him I'll give, ever to Him I'll cling,
In His blessed presence live, ever His praises sing.
Love so mighty and so true merits my soul's best songs;
Faithful, loving service, too, to Him belongs.
Love lifted me (even me)!
Love lifted me (even me)!
When nothing else could help,
Love lifted me!
Souls in danger, look above, Jesus completely saves;
He will lift you by His love, out of the angry waves.
He's the Master of the sea, billows His will obey;
He your Savior wants to be—*be saved today!*
Love lifted me (even me)!
Love lifted me (even me)!
When nothing else could help,
Love lifted me!

Passover
Practical Guide
Introduction

The Sprinkling Of The
Passover Lamb

This practical guide of the Feast of Passover is meant to inspire you with ways to celebrate the feast with your family. It incorporates the specific instruction given by God through Moses with traditions out of the Jewish and Messianic Jewish congregations. In the Bible, you will notice that the instructions from God about Passover shine in their simplicity and clarity (Exodus 12:6–7; Leviticus 23:5–8, 23:9–14).

The first Passover was about following the instructions God had given the Israelites through Moses. As time passed, many traditions and "man-made laws" had developed that were "given by men" about Passover. These laws are captured in the *Mishnah* and *Talmud*. The intention is to emphasize what the Bible teaches and to look at these Jewish traditions that give a greater understanding of God, Jesus Christ, and perhaps, in a limited way, the Jewish culture.

This prompts the question, however, of how Jesus Christ celebrated the Passover feast? The Bible gives us no insight about how Jesus specifically celebrated the feast in regard to Jewish traditions. I am convinced that Jesus Christ celebrated Passover exactly the way it brought the greatest honor and joy to His Father. Moreover, Jesus himself explains that He came not to abolish the law but to fulfill the law. The New Testament emphasizes how Jesus always walked in complete obedience to His Father's will. Jesus was never concerned about fulfilling any of the traditions or man-made laws.

The Days Before Passover
(Tenth Day to the Evening of the Fourteenth Day)

The Israelites were instructed to take a lamb for each family for a sacrifice. It had to be a one-year-old male with no defects. Special care had to be given to this chosen animal until the evening of the fourteenth day of the first month. A perfect white soft woolly lamb comes to live with you! Wonderful! Most of us will not be able to have a real lamb brought into our homes. But how about using a stuffed animal lamb? It will do just fine. Make it a part of any activity in the house. We have a way of getting attached, very quickly, to our pets. Especially children! Younger children may even play with the lamb. Take time with your family to read each day some Bible verses (Luke 22) starting on Palm Sunday. Each one can share how he or she sees these events unfold until Easter (Passover). The lamb will be in your safe keeping until the fourteenth day, the day it will be killed.

Jesus too was loved before He was sacrificed. He was living among them in their homes and families. Pray and ask God to give you insight. Are there any other parallels? Share them with your family.

The Eve Before Passover

A traditional ceremony is held on the evening before Passover. The mother hides pieces of bread (leavened) in the house. After nightfall, the dad takes a wooden spoon and a candle in his hand. At his lead by candlelight, the children follow behind him in search of the hidden bread pieces. When a piece is found, the dad scoops it up with the spoon (to avoid touching it) and places it in a paper bag.

Use this time to focus on what God would show the family. Have we not all sinned and fallen short of the glory of God? Do we walk in darkness until Christ's light reveals to us our sin? What more is God showing us? Share it with the family. Afterward, the entire family can gather to burn the bag with the bread (our sins).

The Evening of Passover

God instructed the Israelites to observe and pass on the Passover ceremony from one generation to the next. God emphasized the importance children have in the Passover Feast by saying that this event shall be observed as an ordinance for you and your children.

The Passover ceremony is called "the Seder" meaning "order." Its intent is to obey the precept "tell your son and daughter." The *Haggadah* is the name given to the text that tells the story in a narrated way of the Exodus. It builds the core of the Seder. Today you can download such texts from the internet. Keep in mind the age of your children so that you use an appropriate text. Such texts can differ in length up to several hours.

You may want to consider texts from the Messianic Jewish community which focus on Jesus Christ. Remember, the intent is not to find the perfect text but to remember and to tell the story. Instead of such special text (Haggadah), you can also just simply use your Bible to tell the story and read passages that God lays upon your heart.

Consider as well that the Israelites were slaves in Egypt. Each family had their own story to tell about being a slave in Egypt. They each had a different story about how it was for them to celebrate the first Passover and how it was for them to experience the many miracles God performed leading them out of slavery to the land flowing with milk and honey.

Our personal story of salvation speaks of how Christ has become our Passover, sacrificed for our sins. This is an opportunity to tell your children of what Jesus did to lead you or your family into the land of milk and honey.

Celebrating Passover "The Seder" With Your Family

The Seder is a family oriented ceremony where everyone gathers around the table. The symbolism associated with the Seder offers a rich experience and a unique way for Christians to meaningfully prepare for Easter. At Passover, the Israelites received freedom from more than 400 years of slavery in Egypt. Passover is revealing a "foreshadowing" of God's plans for Christ's death on the cross and resurrection. The Lamb of God brought us freedom from our slavery to sin.

The Jewish and Messianic Jewish people celebrate the Seder with many additional symbols and traditions that exceed by far the simplicity of God's instructions. While some of these traditions clearly tell the message of Passover and of Jesus Christ, others are, however, from somewhat controversial origins and were therefore not included here.

The following is intended to be an example of how to celebrate the Seder in your family. It incorporates Jewish tradition and prayers from a Christian perspective.

The Passover Seder

The Passover Table

The Passover Table

You find on the Passover Table the Seder plate that carries the symbolic food items. Some Seder plates are beautifully ornate. They are a central part of the Passover table, and something that in Jewish tradition is often passed to the next generation. You also find candles and three loaves of matzah (unleavened bread) on the table. A special napkin sometimes holds this bread, which has a pocket for each loaf. However, a simple cloth napkin will do.

The Lighting of the Candles

The Seder begins with the lighting of the two candles found on a festively set dinner table. This is traditionally done by the mother or the mother and daughter together.

While she lights the <u>first candle</u>, she praises God for bringing forth light out of darkness:

> *For you are a chosen people. You are royal priests, a holy nation, God's very own possession. As a result, you can show others the goodness of God, for he called you out of the darkness into his wonderful light.* (1 Peter 2:9)

With the <u>second candle</u> she states what Jesus said,

> *"I am the light of the world."*

> *Jesus spoke to the people once more and said, "I am the light of the world. If you follow me, you won't have to walk in darkness, because you will have the light that leads to life."* (John 8:12)

After lighting the candles, she waves her hands over the flames three times (as if welcoming in the holiday), and covering her eyes with her hands (so as not to see the candles burning), this traditional Jewish prayer is said:

> *Blessed art Thou, Lord our god, Master of the universe, who sanctifies us with Thy commandments, and commanded us to kindle the light (of the Shabbat and of) the holiday.*

The Four Cups of Wine (Or Grape Juice)

The Seder is divided in sections. Each person will have a glass with wine or grape juice filled for each section of the Seder. These four cups serve to remember the four promises God gave Moses in Exodus.

> Say, therefore, to the sons of Israel, "I am the Lord, and I will bring you out from under the

burdens of the Egyptians, and I will deliver you from their bondage. I will also redeem you with an outstretched arm and with great judgments. Then I will take you for My people, and I will be your God; and you shall know that I am the Lord your God, who brought you out from under the burdens of the Egyptians." (Exodus 6:6–7).

The four cups are[2]:

- Sanctification:
  I will bring you out from under the burdens of the Egyptians.
- Deliverance (or instructions):
  I will free (rescue) you from their bondage (slavery).
- Redemption (or betrothal):
  I will redeem you with an outstretched arm and with great judgments.
- Restoration (or Praise):
  I will take you as my own people and I will be your God.

1. THE FIRST CUP OF WINE (Sanctification)

The Kiddush

The Kiddush, which means consecration, begins by holding up the first cup of wine or grape juice. This is referred to as the cup of sanctification which means to be set apart for God. Remembered here are God's provisions and freedom from slavery. The cup of wine is a symbol of joy (Psalm 104:15) that is ours as a result of our salvation. We remember that Christ set us apart from the world as a holy nation to himself (1 Peter 2:9).

---

[2] Be aware that each section or cup may somewhat differ in its content from one community to the another. In parentheses, you will find other common names given for that particular cup.

In an opening prayer, speak likewise out to God what it means to you to remember your salvation and sanctification in this Passover celebration.

Traditional prayers:

> *Blessed are You LORD, King of the Universe, who made us holy with his commandments and favored us, and gave us His holy Sabbath, in love and favor, to be our heritage, as a memorial of the Creation. It is the foremost day of the holy festivals marking the Exodus from Egypt. For out of all the nations You chose us and made us holy, and You gave us Your holy Sabbath, in love and favor, as our heritage. Blessed are you LORD, who sanctifies the Sabbath.*
>
> *Blessed art thou, Lord our God, Master of the universe, who has kept us alive and sustained us and has brought us to this special time.*
>
> *Blessed art Thou, Lord our God, King of the universe, Creator of the fruit of the vine.*

This first cup represents that God brought Israel out of Egypt and how he chose Israel to be his own treasured people. He had separated Israel and therefore sanctified them.

> *I am the LORD, and I will free you from the burdens of the land of Egypt.*

Everyone drinks now from the first cup.

The Washing of Hands

The washing of hands follows the Kiddush. A pitcher filled with water, a basin, and a towel is passed around the table. Each person will take a turn pouring water over the hands of the one sitting next to him. It is customary to pour some water over the right hand three times, and then over the left hand tree times. This tradition points to the high priest washing before he entered into the Holy of Holies. You may read John 13:4–12 of Jesus (our high priest) washing the disciple's feet.

The Afikoman

Next are the three loaves of unleavened bread (Matzah) on the table that are called a Unity. The three breads are stacked on top of each other. The middle bread is taken and broken in two pieces. One half is wrapped in a napkin and hidden (placed under a pillow). This is called the *Afikoman*, meaning, "that which comes after." The other half is placed back with the other two breads. The three loaves of unleavened bread represent the unity of God the Father, the Son, and the Holy Spirit. The middle piece, Christ, is broken (reminding us of his death). The hiding of the one half symbolizes his burial (more instructions will follow).

Jewish traditions explain that these three Matzah represent Abraham, Isaac, and Jacob. The middle Matzah (representing Isaac) is broken to recall how he was offered himself in obedience to the will of his father. The binding and offering of Isaac (ram) is a prophetic picture of how Jesus yielded himself to be sacrificed by God the Father as the Lamb of God.

Text: Genesis 22:5–18; John 1:29; Hebrews 11:17–19

Traditional prayer:

This is the bread of brokenness which our fathers ate in the land of Egypt. All who are hungry—let them come and eat. All who are needy—let them come and celebrate the Passover with us.

2. THE SECOND CUP OF WINE
(Deliverance or Instruction)

An invitation is given by the leader of the group (usually the father of the family) by lifting up the second cup which is called the cup of deliverance or instruction.

The Four Questions

A reading dialogue begins by the children asking questions. "Why is this night different from all other nights? Why are we eating unleavened bread?" This portrays what is written. Your children will ask you what this ceremony means to you (Exodus 12:24–27).

The leader will reply by telling the story of "remembering" that they were slaves in Egypt. As Christians, this is an opportunity to remember our own distinct story of salvation. Rejoice over what Jesus Christ, your Passover Lamb, did in your life.

There are four traditional questions that the children ask:

A) Why is it that on all other nights during the year we eat either bread or matzah, but on this night we eat only matzah?

Answer: To remember the bread of affliction we had to eat when we were slaves and to remember how our ancestors fled Egypt in such a hurry that they did not have time (remember God's instruction given to Moses).

B) Why is it that on all other nights, we eat all kinds of herbs, but on this night we eat only bitter herbs?

Answer: We eat them to remind ourselves of how our ancestor's lives were bitter as slaves in Egypt.

C) Why is it that on all other nights we do not dip our herbs even once, but on this night we dip them twice?

Answer: We dip them in salt water to remember the salty tears of the slaves and to remember how we crossed the salty waters of the sea. We also dip the *maror* (bitter herb) in the *charoseth* to remember how the bitterness of our slavery was made sweet by the hope for our freedom.

D) Why is it that on all other nights we eat either sitting or reclining, but on this night we eat in a reclining position?

Answer: We recline tonight as a symbol of our freedom, for when we were slaves, we could never recline in comfort.

The Midrash

The leader now tells the story about the miraculous signs God performed which brought judgment on Egypt (Exodus 9:3, 11:4, 12:12).

> **INSIGHT**
>
> *Midrash* means "to investigate" or to "study."

Ten Plagues

1. Blood: All the water was changed to blood.
2. Frogs: An infestation of frogs sprang up in Egypt.
3. Lice: The Egyptians were afflicted by lice.
4. Flies: An infestation by swarms of flies came upon Egypt.
5. Pestilence: A plague killed off the Egyptian livestock.
6. Boils: An epidemic of boils afflicted the Egyptians.
7. Hail: Hail rained from the sky.
8. Locusts: Locusts swarmed over Egypt.
9. Darkness: Egypt was covered in darkness.
10. Killing of the firstborn: All of the Egyptians firstborn sons and firstborn livestock were slain.

Then the leader comes to the part where it is written, "Take some of the blood and put it on the door frames of the houses where they eat the lamb" (Exodus 12:7). Now the leader recites the miracles God performed beginning with parting the sea to the journey in the dessert. To recognize the fact that the Israel complained even after these miracles, the group collectively says, "*We should have been content*" after each miracle mentioned.

God's Miracles During Israel's Journey

1. The miracle of the pillar of cloud and fire.
2. The parting of the See and God's victory over the Egyptian army.
3. The sweetening of the bitter water at Marah.
4. The miracle of the quail.
5. The miracle of the manna (bread) from heaven.
6. The miracle of the life–giving water from the rock.
7. The defeat of the Amalekites at Rephidim.

This is also a time to reflect on our grumbling and where we should be content. What miracles did God perform in our desert? Do we recognize similarities in our behavior that cause us to grumble?

At every stage of the journey out of Egypt to the rendezvous point at Mt. Sinai, God demonstrated His covenant love and His protection of Israel. In this courtship journey, the Israelites learned to trust God to provide for their needs and they learned to be obedient to God's commands (Exodus 16:1–18:27).

The Hallel (Praise)

Next is the first part of the Hallel reading (Psalm 113). You may read alternately between the leader and the family.

Example:

> *Leader: Praise the Lord! Praise, O servants of the Lord.*
> *Family: Praise the name of the Lord.*
> *Leader: Blessed be the name of the Lord.*
> *Family: From this time forth and forever.*
> *Leader: From the rising of the sun to its setting.*
> *Family: The name of the Lord is to be praised…etc.*

Traditional prayer:

> *We were slaves to Pharaoh in Egypt. But the LORD our God brought us out from there by a mighty and outstretched arm.*
>
> *Had the Holy One, blessed be He, not taken out our forefathers from Egypt, then we, our children, and our children's children would still be enslaved to Pharaoh in Egypt!*
>
> *Blessed are Thou, Lord our God, King of the universe, who releases the captives.*

Messianic Jewish prayer:

> *Blessed are You, Lord our God, King of the universe, who gave to us the way of salvation through the Messiah Yeshua, blessed be He, Amen.*

Now the group drink of the second cup.

The Symbolic Meal (Deuteronomy 16:1–8)

Since the destruction of the temple, the Jews have not been able to celebrate the Passover Feast as described by God. The rabbis dealt with this problem by introducing a substitute symbol, a lamb shank bone, for the Passover lamb. So it became tradition to have a shank bone (without any meat) placed on the Passover plate. However, some Messianic Jews might have some lamb meat on the shank bone (see below "sandwich" explanation). There are usually a variety of additional, non-scriptural food symbols found on the Passover plate. The following is a list of the most common symbolic items on the plate:

- Charoseth (Clay):
  This is a mixture of chopped apples with walnuts. Added are sugar, cinnamon, wine, or grape juice all mixed

together. It is to remind the Jews about the clay or mortar they made in Egypt.

- Maror (Bitter):
  Bitter herbs are used to symbolize the bitterness and harshness of the slavery the Israelites endured in Egypt (normally horseradish or romaine lettuce / some use green onion or celery leaves).

- Karpas (Fresh raw vegetable):
  A vegetable (parsley or celery) other than bitter herbs, which is dipped into salt water (which represents tears) mirrors the pain felt by the slavery and to remind them that God brought them across the Red Sea (salt water) into a new land (green vegetable).

- Shank bone:
  A roasted lamb or goat shank bone symbolizes the sacrificed lamb whose blood was put upon the doorposts.

- Beitzah (A roasted hard-boiled egg):
  There are a variety of speculations on how the egg found its way into Passover. Some say that this is a symbol of mourning (as eggs are the first thing served to mourners after a funeral) evoking the idea of mourning over the destruction of the temple and their consequential inability to offer sacrifices for Passover. It is normally not eaten during the formal part of the Seder but rather as the first course of the meal by having the hard-boiled egg dipped in saltwater.

- Bowl of salt water:
  See above explanation for *Karpas*.

You may find several other symbolic food items on the Passover plate that are not listed here. The intention is that with each item, a symbolic value is explained. They are used to tell the story. As each story is told, everyone eats a small portion of that particular symbolic food. Except, of course, the shank bone! If you decided to have some meat on the shank bone, it is tradition to make a sandwich of *matzah*, *maror* (bitter herbs), and lamb meat to fulfill what God commanded in Exodus.

> That same night, they must roast the meat
> over a fire and eat it along with bitter salad greens
> and bread made without yeast (Exodus 12:8).

After a prayer of thanksgiving and praise, the unleavened bread is broken (not the hidden piece of bread) and passed around so that all may partake.

Traditional prayer:

> *Blessed are You. Lord our God, King of the universe, who sanctified us with his commandments, and commanded us to eat matzah.*

A Festive Dinner

After the symbolic meal, a festive dinner is eaten. Some of the typical dishes are matzo ball soup, noodles with poppy seeds, roasted lamb, salad, Passover cake.

Jews have an extra place setting for Elijah at the dinner table. They believe that Elijah will come at Passover. We know that Elijah has come. Our hope is in Jesus Christ. He is the hope for a lost world.

> Then his disciples asked him, "Why do the
> teachers of religious law insist that Elijah must return
> before the Messiah comes?" Jesus replied, "Elijah is
> indeed coming first to get everything ready. But
> I tell you, Elijah has already come, but he wasn't
> recognized, and they chose to abuse him. And in

the same way they will also make the Son of Man suffer." Then the disciples realized he was talking about John the Baptist. (Matthew 17:10–13)

Traditional Prayer after the Dinner

Blessed are you, Lord our God, master of the universe, who nourishes the whole world in goodness, with grace, kindness, and compassion. He gives bread to all flesh, for His love endures forever. And though his great goodness we have never lacked, nor will we lack food forever, for the sake of His great Name. For He is God, who nourishes and sustains all, and does good to all, and prepares food for all His creatures which He created. Blessed are You, Lord, who nourishes all. Amen.

The Seder Continues with the Afikoman

The children will now enjoy finding the hidden piece of matzo (Afikoman) which is hidden behind a pillow. As portrayed earlier, the Messianic Jews point here to Jesus Christ. The loaf was broken in the beginning, showing the breaking of the body of Jesus Christ.

For I received from the Lord that which I also delivered to you: that the Lord Jesus on the same night in which He was betrayed took bread; and when He had given thanks, He broke it and said, "Take, eat; this is My body which is broken for you; do this in remembrance of Me." (1 Corinthians 11:23–24)

Geneva Study Bible: This word broken denotes to us the manner of Christ's death, for although his legs were not broken, as the thieves' legs were, yet his body was very severely tormented, and torn, and bruised.

Like Jesus was wrapped in linen after he died on the cross, so is the loaf wrapped in linen. His burial is symbolized by hiding the loaf behind the pillow. The angel of the Lord removed the stone portrayed by the removal of the pillow. The loaf is then unwrapped, picturing Jesus's resurrection. Now the loaf is broken into pieces for each person celebrating the Passover. We are eating the bread of life, the perfect sacrifice for our sins. Each person needs to "find" Jesus Christ, their Afikoman.

> Jesus said, "I tell you the truth, Moses didn't give you bread from heaven. My Father did. And now he offers you the true bread from heaven. The true bread of God is the one who comes down from heaven and gives life to the world." (John 6:32–33)

> This is my body given for you; do this in remembrance of me. (Luke 22:19)

Everyone eats a piece of the Afikoman—the unleavened bread.

 ## 3. THE THIRD CUP OF WINE (Redemption)

The *Mishnah* says the wine in this cup recalls the shed blood of the lamb that was applied to the doorposts in Egypt, causing the plague of death to pass over. The sacrificial lamb offered on Passover paid the price to deliver the nation of Israel from the bondage of Egypt.

Jesus Christ himself associated this cup with the blood he would shed on the cross, causing death to "pass over" those trusting in him. This is the cup of the new covenant, that is, God's new agreement to regard all those who trust in the death of the Messiah for the forgiveness of their sins to be justified and made right with Him.

After supper he took another cup of wine and said, "This cup is the new covenant between God and his people—an agreement confirmed with my blood, which is poured out as a sacrifice for you." (Luke 22:20)

But by His doing you are in Christ Jesus, who became to us wisdom from God, and righteousness and sanctification, and redemption. (1 Corinthians 1:30)

At this time, a prayer of praise is spoken for God's provision of redemption. The third cup is then drank from—the cup of redemption.

4. THE FOURTH CUP OF WINE (Restoration or Praise)

The final cup is a cup of praise and a reminder of God's promise to Israel:

I will take you as my own people. (Exodus 6:7)

The Jewish people look forward to an age when everyone will be at peace and will be reunited with God.

Traditional prayer:

O Israel, trust in the Lord! He is their help and their shield! O house of Aaron, trust in the Lord! He is their help and their shield! You who fear the Lord, trust in the Lord! He is their help and their shield!

The Hallel (the second part)

Read Psalm 115 and 118 (You may read Psalm 118 alternately between the leader and the family)

All recite Revelation 5:12–13.

> *And they sang in a mighty chorus: "Worthy is the Lamb who was slaughtered—to receive power and riches and wisdom and strength and honor and glory and blessing." And then I heard every creature in heaven and on earth and under the earth and in the sea. They sang: "Blessing and honor and glory and power belong to the one sitting on the throne and to the Lamb forever and ever."* (Revelation 5:12–13)

Be part of God's wonderful plan to bring the Good News of Jesus Christ into a desperate world. Think about it. You will bring hope in someone's life that will change their presence and future.

Consider what is written:

> Then the eleven disciples left for Galilee, going to the mountain where Jesus had told them to go. When they saw him, they worshiped him—but some of them doubted! Jesus came and told his disciples, "I have been given all authority in heaven and on earth. Therefore, go and make disciples of all the nations, baptizing them in the name of the Father and the Son and the Holy Spirit. Teach these new disciples to obey all the commands I have given you. And be sure of this: I am with you always, even to the end of the age." (Matthew 28:16–20)

This fourth cup represents our great hope as Christians that the Messiah will return soon!

> As they strained to see him rising into heaven, two white–robed men suddenly stood among them. "Men of Galilee," they said, "why are you standing here staring into heaven? Jesus has been taken from you into heaven, but someday he will return from heaven in the same way you saw him go!" (Acts 1:10–11)

Let us now joyfully drink from the fourth cup.

> I will lift up the cup of salvation and praise the Lord's name for saving me. (Psalm 116:13)

The Priestly Blessing (Numbers 6:22–27)

In conclusion of the Seder, the father speaks the following over his family:

> *Then the Lord said to Moses, "Tell Aaron and his sons to bless the people of Israel with this special blessing: 'May the Lord bless you and protect you. May the Lord smile on you and be gracious to you. May the Lord show you his favor and give you his peace.' Whenever Aaron and his sons bless the people of Israel in my name, I myself will bless them."*

The Seder always concludes by saying in unison this traditional and joyful phrase:

> *Until next year in Jerusalem!*

The Omer
The Counting of the Fifty Days

The counting of the days is rooted in the Torah's command found in Leviticus 23. It is not a festival but a command that sets the time between two festivals. The fifty day countdown to Pentecost begins the day after the Sabbath Passover (second day of Passover).

In Jewish tradition, the seven weeks before Pentecost are called "Counting the Omer (Omer: biblical measure of barley)." During the temple period on each of these days, a priest would wave a sheaf of barley before the Lord as a symbolic gesture of dedicating the coming harvest to Him. On the fiftieth day (Pentecost), a sample of the first crop of the wheat harvest was baked into two loaves of leavened bread and waved before the altar as the climax of the season.

The two festivals of Passover and Pentecost are linked together by these forty-nine days. Pentecost is regarded as the culmination of the experience of redemption, sometimes called the "Conclusion of Passover." Just as the redemption by the blood of the lambs led to Israel's deliverance and the giving of the Torah at Sinai, so the redemption by the blood of Jesus Christ led to deliverance and the giving of the Holy Spirit at Zion. Just as Moses had waited before the Torah was given to Israel, so the disciples waited before the Holy Spirit was given.

INSIGHT

A WORD OF CAUTION

The Omer has been for some Jews a time of semi-mourning. Traditionally, the reason cited is the event in memory of the Bar Kochba revolt against the Romans where a plague killed 24,000 students of Rabbi Akiva who is referred to in the *Talmud* as Head of all the Sages (wise men). He also was a leading contributor to the *Mishnah*. There exists, however, a disagreement that it was not a plague but that the Romans killed these students. However, this tragedy came to pass during the counting of the Omer.

Semi-mourning means that no weddings or other festivities are held nor music is heard and no hair is cut. The mourning continued to the thirty-third day of the Omer, which is considered to be the day in which the plague was lifted (or the fighting had ceased). Others proceed to mourn until the thirty-fourth day which is regarded by them to be the day of joy and celebration.

Bar Kochba was the leader of the Jewish army through the revolt dating 132–135 AD and was regarded by many Jews as the Messiah who could restore Israel. Some even hoped for a rebuilding of the temple. The lost revolt instead resulted in a ban on Jews entering Jerusalem by the Romans and in the building of a temple to Zeus on the former Temple Mount.

Rabbi Akiva's false belief that Bar Kochba was the Messiah led to the needless death of thousands of Jews. It stirred up a great persecution among Jewish believers in Jesus that did not take up arms against the Romans on behalf of this false Messiah, Bar Kochba. Since they protested, they were considered traitors to the Jewish state and were shut out by their fellow Jews.

Simeon Rabbi Yochai has been a famous disciple of Rabbi Akiva. This celebration of the thirty-third day of the Omer Count is a holiday called Lag B'Omer. It commemorates the death of Rabbi Bar Yochai.

The Zohar (splendor or radiance) is the foundational work in the literature of Jewish mystical thought known as Kabbalah. It first appeared in Spain in the thirteenth century and was published by a Jewish writer named Moses de León. He ascribed the work to Bar Yochai who, according to Jewish legend, hid in a cave for thirteen years studying the Torah and was inspired by the Prophet Elijah to write the Zohar. This accords with the traditional claim by adherents that Kabbalah is the concealed part of the Oral Torah.

While the traditional majority view in religious Judaism has been that the teachings of Kabbalah were revealed by God to biblical figures such as Abraham and Moses and were then transmitted orally from the biblical era until its redaction by Bar Yochai, modern academic analysis of the Zohar, such as that by the twentieth century religious historian, Gershon Scholem, has theorized that De León was the actual author.

The view of non-Orthodox Jewish denominations generally conforms to this latter view, and as such, most non-Orthodox Jews have long viewed the Zohar as *pseudepigrapha* and *apocrypha* while sometimes accepting that its contents may have meaning for modern Judaism. Jewish prayer books edited by non-Orthodox Jews may therefore contain excerpts from the Zohar and other Kabbalistic works, even if the editors do not literally believe that they are oral traditions from the time of Moses.

Why an Omer?

Although there is nothing specific mentioned in the Bible of a "counting of an Omer," there are some possible explanations. On the Feast of First Fruits, a wave offering was presented of a sheaf from the first fruits of the harvest. The Hebrew word for a sheaf is *omer* (Leviticus 23:10–11). At Pentecost (Shavuot), another first fruits offering is presented, this time a wave offering made of two-tenths of an *ephah*; they shall be of fine flour baked with leaven as first fruits to Yahveh. Two-tenths of an ephah is equal to two omers, two loaves of bread made of one omer of fine flour each (Leviticus 23:17). Hence we find that the counting from Pentecost toward Shavuot is from one omer to another.

Furthermore, there is a connection in the amount of manna that was gathered each day by the Israelites in the desert. They were told before receiving manna for the first time that they ought to gather one omer per person (Exodus 16:16–18). This was their daily provision. The omer, measuring 2.2 liters, is the amount of food needed for a person to be properly nourished for a day. The focus was on what God provided and not what the Israelites were able to earn by their own hands and hard work. It is a beautiful way of seeing our daily provision by God by reminding us to look to His blessings and His provision each day.

Counting the omer outlines the journey of the Israelites from Egypt through the desert wasteland to the revelation of God at Mount Sinai where He gave the Commandments through Moses and where He made a Covenant with His people Israel. It was on this journey that God revealed the Sabbath day to His people and satisfied their hunger with manna from heaven (Exodus16). When they complained of thirst, He caused water to spring forth. Each day, the Israelites—"the people of God"— were commanded to count the Omer as they experienced their way out from Egypt. When Israel set off, they left behind hundreds of years of Egyptian influence, idolatry, and the slave mentality they had developed as they were oppressed and driven by harsh taskmasters. But at the height of suffering, God sent Moses to bring them out of their bondage by leading them to freedom.

The Israelites, who were redeemed by the blood of the Passover lamb, left Egypt forever and took on a new life and a new leader. In effect, a nation of slaves was now a nation of freed men. For the Israelites, the journey through the wilderness was a time of trial and testing. Deeply engraved was a mindset of bondage from their slavery in Egypt. At every stage of the journey out of Egypt to the rendezvous point at Mt. Sinai, God demonstrated His covenant love and His protection of Israel. The Israelites were learning to trust God to provide for their needs and to be obedient to His commands.

God performed many miracles on the courtship journey with Israel to the rendezvous at Mount Sinai:

- The pillar of cloud and fire to lead Israel (Exodus 13:21–22).
- The parting of the Red Sea and God's victory over the Egyptian army (Exodus 14:13–31).

> Be aware that Kabbalah is a deceptive system of thought that seduces people into denying that they are sinners in need of salvation. For the Kabbalist, human nature is essentially asleep or in a state of forgetfulness regarding its divine origin.
>
> People are really made in the image of God, which for a Kabbalist means that each of us are essentially divine beings. Each soul is a miniature version of God Himself, like a fragmented holographic image. Human beings are not totally depraved or victims of original sin but are rather covered up with shells that need to be removed so that the original spark of God can shine through. Every soul is pure in essence, and the only salvation to speak of is to become enlightened, to remember the truth of who and what we really are.
>
> In conclusion, note that many Messianic Jews earnestly urge Christians and Jews not to celebrate this Log B'Omer holiday. Their reasons of concern are reflected in the explanations found above. They continue by stating that this holiday is not a commanded holiday.

- The Lord provides water at Marah (Exodus 15:22–27).
- The Lord provides manna (bread) from heaven (Exodus 16:1–7).
- The Lord provides meat (Exodus 16:8–21).
- The life-giving water in the rock (Exodus 17:1–7).
- The defeat of the Amalekites at Rephidim (Exodus 16:8–16).

The Day of the Omer Count

For a Jew, the counting of each day represents a spiritual preparation and anticipation for the giving of the Torah on Mount Sinai. It is a time of spiritual reflection, growth, and purification. Thus the counting of the Omer demonstrates how much a Hebrew desires to accept the Torah in his own life. Many Jews also pray a prayer for the final redemption of God's people at this time, praying for the Messiah to come quickly, to restore the temple speedily, and to make it possible to reinstate the observance of the Omer offering and counting at the temple.

Jewish ritual requires that after nightfall, the one who is counting the omer recites the following blessing (approximately thirty minutes after sundown):

> *Baruch atah A-donai E-loheinu Melekh Ha-olam asher kid'shanu b'mitzvotav v'tzivanu al S'firat Ha-omer.*

Translation:

> *Blessed are You, Lord our God, King of the Universe, Who has sanctified us with His commandments and commanded us to count the Omer.*

Next is the count of the omer by saying,

> *Today is the _____ week of the Omer count,*
> *and the _____ day of the week, making _____*
> *days in all. Therefore, there are _____ days till the*
> *Feast of Pentecost.*

Tradition prescribes the recitation of Psalm 67 since it is composed of exactly seven verses and forty-nine words in Hebrew which corresponds to the seven weeks and forty-nine days of the omer count. The Psalm is also seasonally appropriate because of its harvest motif. It is spiritually appropriate because it speaks clearly of God's salvation being made known over all the earth.

Christians and the Counting of the Omer

> God wonderfully provided a cloud to lead Israel out of Egypt (Exodus 13:17–22). He used Moses to part the Red Sea and enabled Israel to escape the pursuing Egyptians who then drowned in the water when God closed it over them (Exodus 14:1–31).

> Paul interprets these events as analogous of being "baptized into Christ" (Romans 6:3; Galatians 3:27).

> Moreover, brethren, I do not want you to be unaware that all our fathers were under the cloud, all passed through the sea, all were baptized into Moses (*into Moses, into the covenant of which Moses was the mediator*) in the cloud and in the sea. (1 Corinthians 10:1–2)

Israel's journey through the wilderness bears within a picture of our Christian life. We too have left behind the sins and idolatries of our own Egypt and turned to Christ. After our baptism, we walk boldly forward while we meet obstacles, confront problems, face trials and difficulties. In other words, we encounter life impacted by the spiritual wilderness of this evil world.

All of the post-resurrection appearances of Jesus recorded in the Bible fell within the days of the omer count. Some Christians use this countdown to have a daily time of reflection about their own personal spiritual life. The stories of Christ's appearances provide plenty of material for a promising start. The goal is that it would lead you to a joyful anticipation to the giving of the Holy Spirit at Pentecost.

This may also be a perfect opportunity to have a forty-nine days of daily family devotion reflecting this season of the omer count. Gather your family after sundown. Pray the Jewish prayer, speak out the omer count and read Psalm 67. Get to know each member of your family better by sharing and listening to what is special to them about the omer count or about Jesus's post resurrection appearances. Make the evening age-appropriate for the children. Involve them by giving them an active part and see were God leads you.

Forty Days of Post-Resurrection Appearances

- The Resurrection Morning:
  Matthew 28:1–10
  Luke 23:56 – 24:12
  Mark 16:1–11
  John 20:1–18

- The Walk to Emmaus
  Mark 16:12–13
  Luke 24:13–35

- To the Disciples in Jerusalem (Thomas being absent)
  Mark 16:14
  Luke 24:36–43
  John 20:19–25

- To Thomas with the Other Disciples Present
  John 20:26–29

- To the Seven Disciples by the Sea of Galilee
  John 21:1–24

- To the Eleven on a Mountain in Galilee
  Matthew 28:14–20
  Mark 16:15–18

- Christ's Final Appearance and His Ascension
  Mark 16:19–20
  Luke 24:44–53
  Acts 1:1–14

- Christ Appeared to Saul (Paul) on the Road to Damascus:
  Acts 9:3–6
  Acts 26:13–18
  Refer to: 1 Corinthians 15:8

- The Fact of Christ's Resurrection (Paul)
  1 Corinthians 15:3–8

CHAPTER 4

INTERMEZZO I

Getting to Know Our Triune God

The consequence of Israel's persistent disobedience and grumbling on their journey in the wilderness resulted in a greater loss of lives than in all the battles combined while conquering "the promised land." Their actions often revealed old thinking patterns and wrong ideas or pictures about God. How Israel sometimes viewed God can best be contrasted with the faith demonstrated by Caleb and Joshua after they scouted out the promised land. Their thinking, action, desire, and determination were marked and led by their trust in God. Everything about it clearly proclaimed and testified to God's love, greatness, and faithfulness (Numbers 14:9–12, 26–38).

And what about Jesus Christ? Did He experience a time of testing? We find that Jesus spent forty days fasting in the wilderness after His baptism. It is recorded that angels came to serve Jesus after Lucifer tested Him and left. What a wonderful expression of how caring and always present our Father God's love is. Do you expect miracles in your wilderness?

Are we ready to enter into God's courtship journey in this time of the Omer? Are we willing to recognize and count the omer, God's blessings, and provisions day by day? Are we willing to turn away from our old habits and thinking patterns? And what about God? Do we really know God and have faith in Him like Joshua or Caleb did? Knowing him is more than head knowledge. It is much more. It is a "knowing" that is seen by Jesus Christ's love to the Father and recognizable by communion with

Him. The Apostle John, who enjoyed remarkably close communion with Jesus, wrote in his letter:

> What we have seen and heard we proclaim to you also, so that you too may have fellowship with us; and indeed our fellowship is with the Father, and with His Son Jesus Christ. These things we write, so that our joy may be made complete. (1 John 1:3–4)

Father, Son, and Holy Spirit may communicate with us "distinctly" in the sense that we may be able to discern each one. Distinctly does not mean "separately." Fellowship with each person of the Trinity is always one facet of ongoing communion with all three. We speak to God the Father, on the basis of Christ's work, by the help of the Holy Spirit. This speaking is called prayer. It is the response of our heart to God in words. It may include our confessions of sin (1 John 1:9), our praises of God's perfections (Psalm 96:4), our thanks for God's gifts (Psalm 118:21), and our requests that he would help us (Psalm 38:22) and others (Romans 15:30–31)—all to the glory of God (Psalm 50:15). Furthermore, our prayer may be in private (Matthew 6:6) or in public (1 Corinthians 14:16). It may last all night (Luke 6:12) or be summed up in a moment's cry (Matthew 14:30). It may be desperate (Jonah 2:2) or joyful (Psalm 119:162). It may be full of faith (Mark 11:24) or wavering with uncertainty (Mark 9:24). But it is not optional. It is commanded, which is good news, because it means that God loves being the source of help and rescue (Psalm 28:7, 50:15).

The Bible reminds us that ordinary people can accomplish great things through prayer (James 5:17–18). It tells us about great answers to prayer (Isaiah 37:21, 36). It gives us wonderful examples of how to pray (Matthew 6:9–13; Ephesians 3:14–19). And it offers amazing encouragement to pray (Matthew 7:7–11).

In our prayer, we express our longing that God's name be hallowed in all the world (Matthew 6:9); that the church would be filled with the fruit of righteousness to the glory and praise of God

(Philippians 1:11); and that the gospel would spread and awaken faith in Jesus among all the nations (Thessalonians 3:1) so that many who do not believe would be saved (Romans 10:1).

The Bible shows that prayer is near the heart of God. When we pray for God to do what only he can do, he gets the *glory* while we get the *joy* (gladness, delight).

> Whatever you ask in My name, that will I do, so that the Father may be glorified in the Son. (John 14:13)

> Until now you have asked for nothing in My name; ask and you will receive, so that your joy may be made full (*complete*). (John 16:24)

Prayer is not a one-way talk to a distant God. It is entering into the throne room of God by the shed blood of the lamb and having a personal talk with God Almighty, your Father. Know that in prayer, God enjoys speaking to your heart. With this thought, I will pause for a moment. Not every thought, impression, emotion, dream, or vision we receive or experience is from God. Therefore, we need to determine that what I am experiencing is actually coming from the Holy Spirit (from God) and not from "myself" or an "evil spirit." In essence, that means if it comes:

- from myself: these experiences are self-directed.
- from an evil spirit: these experiences line up with any of the names of Lucifer.
- from God: these experiences line up with any of the names of our Triune God.

The Bible teaches us to be active and:

Test to determine the source. Test the spirit! (1 John 4:1).

- Your mind is most likely in an empty idle stage when you receive something "from Lucifer." Such thoughts are most commonly obstructive. Bind and rebuke those coming from him in the Name of Jesus Christ.
- Those coming from "myself" should be rejected, because what you really want in your life is Jesus in action through you, not yourself in action.
- You most likely receive "from God" when your inner being is quiet and focused on Jesus Christ.

Examine its content. Test the Idea! (1 John 4:5).

- If the content comes from Lucifer, it will be negative, destructive, pushy, fearful, accusative, violating the nature of God, violating the Word of God, resisting, or afraid to be tested. It will, however, be very appealing to your fleshly desires and ego.
- In contrast, the content from God will be instructive, uplifting, comforting, and it will accept testing.

See Its Fruit. Test the fruit! (Matthew 7:15–20).

- From Lucifer you will find the fruit of fear, compulsion, bondage, anxiety, confusion, condemnation, addictions, and it will have inflated your ego.
- If it is from God, the fruit will be faith, power, peace, wisdom, conviction, revelation, knowledge, and humility.

How should you then enter into communion with God? Here are some recommendations:

Start by recognizing that we need to quiet ourselves. It is written, "My soul, wait in silence for God only, For my hope is from Him" (Psalm 62:5). We are living in a fast-paced world. If you are distracted about something that you need to do, simply write it down so you don't forget. Or maybe you are reminded of sins that need to be confessed. Repent and clothe yourself with the robe of righteousness.

Worship works for many to quiet themselves. Personally, doing things outside and enjoying nature helps me to quiet myself. Find what helps you. It is critical that you focus on Jesus Christ. The Bible teaches us to fix our eyes upon Jesus. God speaks to our heart often in a gentle way that could, if we're not careful, quickly be ignored by our will. However, if we embrace His voice, it will cause in us a sense of excitement, conviction, faith, awe, or peace. His speaking carries with it the strength to carry out what He tells us as well the joy of doing so.

Next, what we experience must line up with the Word of God. We need to pray and see if we feel a sense of peace in our heart about it (Colossians 3:15). Do not neglect the value of confirmation by a mature Christian you trust (Proverbs 11:13). Don't expose an attitude of "God told me so!" All revelation is to be tested. Mistakes are inevitable if we are serious about growing in Christ. Such growth calls for time spent in the Bible. Pray that God will use His Word to bring new life to you by His Spirit.

With these things in place, we often marvel how personally the Bible speaks to us. However, the words in the Bible pointedly address the concerns of long ago people in faraway places facing specific problems, many of which no longer exist. They had no difficulty seeing their application. Much of what they read spoke to actual situations they were facing. Yet, the Bible repeatedly affirms that these words are also written for us.

Whatever was written in former days was written for our instruction (Romans 15:4; Deuteronomy 29:29; 1 Corinthians 10:11; 2 Timothy 3:15–17). Application today discovers ways in which the Holy Spirit reapplies scripture in a timely fashion. The Bible was written to others but speaks to you. The Bible is about God but draws you in. Your challenge is always to reapply scriptures afresh, because God's purpose is always to rescript your life.

When Jesus opened the disciple's minds to understand the scriptures (Luke 24:45), He showed how everything written in the

Bible revealed Himself. At the same time, Jesus demonstrates how He includes us within His own story.

God communicates with us in many ways through the Bible and seeks the response of our communion with Him. If God convicts us (2 Corinthians 7:8–10), we respond by allowing and seeking sorrow and repentance. If He commends us (Psalm 18:19–29), we declare God's greatness and look to Him and resolve to obey and overcome by His strength and grace working within us (we are the temple of the Holy Spirit). If He makes a promise (Hebrew 13:5–6), we place our trust and faith in Him. If He warns us of some danger (Luke 21:34), we take Him seriously and listen to His instruction with a thankful heart knowing of His presence. If He reveals something new about Himself (Isaiah 46:9–11), His Son (Mark 1:11), or His Holy Spirit (John 16:13–14), we affirm it and marvel about His grace at work.

Recognize that the Holy Spirit can speak to us personally through the Word of God. His word opens up the way to grow in relationship with our Triune God on our journey with Him. Names are given in the Bible for a specific reason. They often reveal one's character. Consequently, the names of our God can become very precious because they reveal and express a part of His being. I invite you to ponder these verses that state the names and attributes of our Triune God. Read and pray with the expectation that God will reveal Himself to you.

Names and Attributes of Jesus Christ (KJV)

Advocate	1 John 2:1
All in All	Ephesians 1:23
Almighty	Revelation 1:8
Alpha and Omega	Revelation 1:8;, 22:13
Amen / The Amen	Revelation 3:14
Anointed One	John 1:41
Apostle of our Profession	Hebrew 3:1
Arm of the Lord	Isaiah. 51:9;, 53:1
Author and Finisher of our Faith	Hebrew 12:2

Author of Eternal Salvation	Hebrews 5:9
Beginning and Ending	Revelation 1:8
Beginning of the Creation of God	Revelation 3:14
Beloved One	Matthew 12:18
Beloved Son	Mark 1:11
Blessed and only Potentate	1 Timothy 6:15
Branch	Isaiah 4:2
Branch of Righteousness	Jeremiah 33:15
Bread of Heaven	John 6:32
Bread of God	John 6:33
Bread of Life	John 6:35
Bridegroom	Matthew 9:15; John 3:29
Captain of Salvation	Hebrew 2:10
Chief Shepherd	1 Peter 5:4
Christ / The Anointed / The Messiah	John 1:41
Christ of God	Luke 9:20
Consolation of Israel	Luke 2:25
Cornerstone	Psalm 118:22; Mark 12:10
Counselor	Isaiah 9:6
Creator	John 1:3
Dayspring/Sunrise from on High	Luke 1:78
Deliverer	Romans 11:26
Desire of all Nations	Haggai 2:7
Door	John 10:7
Elect of God	Isaiah 42:1
Everlasting Father	Isaiah 9:6
Emmanuel, God with us	Matthew 1:23
Faithful and True One	Revelation 19:11
Faithful Witness	Revelation 1:5
First and Last	Revelation 1:17
First Begotten / Firstborn of the Dead	Revelation 1:5
Forerunner	Hebrews 6:20

Glory of the Lord	Isaiah 40:5
God	Isaiah 40:3; John 20:28
God Blessed Forever	Romans 9:5
God the Only Begotten Son	John 1:18
Good Shepherd	John 10:11
Governor / Ruler	Matthew 2:6
Great High Priest	Hebrew 4:14
Head of all Things	Ephesians 1:22
Head of the Church	1 Peter 5:4; Colossians 1:18
Heir of all Things	Hebrew 1:2
Holy Child / Holy Servant	Acts 4:27
Holy One	Acts 3:14
Holy One of God	Mark 1:24
Holy One of Israel	Isaiah 41:14
Horn of Salvation	Luke 1:69
Intercessor / Advocate	1 John 2:1
Image of God	2 Corinthians 4:4
Immanuel	Isaiah 7:14
Jesus Christ (Messiah)	Matthew 1:1
Jesus / Yeshua	Matthew 1:21
Jesus of Nazareth	Matthew 21:11
Jesus Son of Joseph	John 1:45
Judge of Israel	Micah 5:1
Judge of the Living and the Dead	Acts 10:42
Just One	Acts 7:52
King	Zechariah 9:9
King of the Ages	1 Timothy 1:17
King of Israel	Mark 15:32
King of the Jews	Matthew 2:2
King of Kings	1 Timothy 6:15
King of the Saints	Revelation 15:3
Lamb	Revelation 13:8
Lamb of God	John 1:29
Last Adam	1 Corinthians 15:45

Lawgiver	Isaiah 33:22
Leader and Commander	Isaiah 55:4
The Life	John 14:6
Light of the World	John 8:12
Lion of the Tribe of Judah	Revelation 5:5
Lord / The Lord	Romans 10:9
Lord of All	Acts 10:36
Lord of Glory	1 Corinthians 2:8
Lord of Lords	1 Timothy 6:15
Lord our Righteousness	Jeremiah 23:6
Master / My great Master / Rabbi	Matthew 23:8
Man of Sorrows	Isaiah 53:3
Mediator	1 Timothy 2:5
Messenger of the Covenant	Malachi 3:1
Messiah	Daniel 9:25; John 1:41
Messiah of God	Luke 9:20
Mighty God	Isaiah 9:6
Mighty One	Isaiah 60:16
Morning Star	Revelation 22:16
Mystery of God	Colossians 2:2
Nazarene	Matthew 2:23
Only Begotten Son	John 1:18
Our Passover	1 Corinthians 5:7
Power of God	1 Corinthians 1:24
Prince of the Kings of the Earth	Revelation 1:5
Price of Life	Acts 3:15
Prince of Peace	Isaiah 9:6
Prophet	Luke 24:19,; Acts 3:22
Rabbi / Teacher / My great Master	Matthew 23:8
Redeemer	Job 19:25
Resurrection and Life	John 11:25
Rejected Stone	Mark 12:10
Rock	1 Corinthians 10:4
Root of David	Revelation 22:16
Rose of Sharon	Song of Solomon 2:1

Righteous One	Acts 3:14
Savior	Luke 2:11
Savior of all Men	1 Timothy 4:10
Savior of the World	John 4:42,;
	Philippians 3:20
Seed of Abraham	Galatians 3:16
Seed of Woman	Genesis 3:15
Shepherd and Bishop of Souls	1 Peter 2:25
Shiloh	Genesis 49:10
Son of Abraham	Matthew 1:1;
	Luke 3:34, 19:9
Son of the Blessed	Mark 14:61
Son of David	Matthew 1:1
Son of the Father	2 John 1:3
Son of the Living God	Matthew 16:16;
	John 6:69
Son of God	Matthew 2:15, 8:29
Son of the Highest	Luke 1:32
Son of Man	Matthew 8:20
Sun of Righteousness	Malachi 4:2
The Coming One	Luke 7:19
The Last Adam	1 Corinthians 15:45
The Living One	Luke 24:5
The Way	John 14:6
True and Righteous Witness	Revelations 3:14
True Light	John 1:9
True Vine	John 15:1
Truth	John 14:6
Watcher of our Souls	1 Peter 2:25
Wisdom of God	1 Corinthians 1:24
Witness	Isaiah 55:4
Word / The Word of God	John 1:1
Word of God	Revelation 19:13
Word of Life	1 John 1:1
Yeshua / Jesus	Matthew 1:21

Names and Attributes of God

We learn about God's Name in Exodus which states:

> But Moses protested, "If I go to the people of
> Israel and tell them, 'The God of your ancestors
> has sent me to you,' they will ask me, 'What is
> his name?' Then what should I tell them?" God
> replied to Moses, "I Am Who I Am. Say this to
> the people of Israel: I Am has sent me to you."
> God also said to Moses, "Say this to the people of
> Israel: Yahweh, the God of your ancestors—the
> God of Abraham, the God of Isaac, and the God
> of Jacob—has sent me to you. This is my eternal
> name, my name to remember for all generations.
> (Exodus 3:13–15 NLT)

"I Am That I Am" (KJV). The words express absolute, and therefore an unchanging and eternal being. Some Bible translations render "I Am Who I Am." Luther renders "I Will Be That I Will Be."

Hebrew Names and Attributes Of God

Adonai Lord or My Lord	Exodus 4:10–12, NAB
Adonai Elohim The Lord God (This Name shows that the source of all being is also the personal God and creator of the entire universe)	Genesis 2:4
Adonai Elohai The Lord My God	Psalm 13:3
YHWH / Yahweh LORD	Exodus 3:13–15

YHWH-Yireh The Lord Will Provide	Genesis 22:13–14
YHWH-Rapha The Lord that Healeth	Exodus 15:26
YHWH-Nissi The Lord Our Banner	Exodus 17:15
YHWH-Shalom The Lord Our Peace	Judges 6:24
YHWH-Tsidkenu The Lord Our Righteousness Our Saving Justice	Jeremiah 23:6
YHWH-Shammah The Lord Is There / The Lord is Present	Ezekiel 48:35
YHWH-Sabaoth The Lord of the Hosts of Heaven	James 5:4
YHWH-Mekoddishkem The Lord Who Sanctifies You	Exodus 31:12
El God (Basic form / The name for God meaning: strength, might or power.)	
El Echad The One God	Malachi 2:10
El Hanne"eman The Faithful God (From *aman*; to support, nourish.)	Deuteronomy 7:9
El Emet The God of Truth (*Emet* means firmness, faithfulness, reliability)	Psalms 31:5
El Tsaddik The Righteous God (Tsaddik means just, righteous)	Isaiah 45:21

El Elyon The Most High God (This title stresses God's strength, sovereignty, and supremacy as Elyon)	Genesis 14:18–20,; Psalms 9:2
El Olam God Everlasting / The Everlasting God (*Olam* means world, universe, everlasting time or space)	Genesis 21:33,; Psalms 90:1–3
El Roi God Who Sees Me	Genesis 16:13–14
El Yeshurun The God of Jeshurun (*Yeshurun* means "the righteous people:" Israel's ideal character and high calling)	Deuteronomy 32:15
El Gibbor The Mighty God (Picture of God as a warrior and champion)	Isaiah 9:6
El De"ot The God of Knowledge (God has perfect knowledge of all things from beginning to end; omniscient)	1 Samuel 2:3
El Haggadol The Great (awesome) God	Deuteronomy 10:17
El Hakkavod The God of Glory	Psalms 29:3
El Hakkadosh The Holy God	Isaiah 5:16
El Hashamayim The God of the Heavens (refers to the abode of God)	Psalms 136:26
El Chaiyai The God of My Life	Psalms 42:8

El Channun The Gracious God	Jonah 4:2
El Yisrael The God Of Israel	Psalms 68:36
El Sali The God of My Strength / God My Rock	Psalms 42:9
El Erekh Apayim avi ha–tanchumim The God of all Patience and Consolation	Romans 15:5
El Rachum The God of Compassion	Deuteronomy 4:31
El Yeshuati The God of My Salvation (*Yeshuah* meaning salvation, deliverance, and victory)	Isaiah 12:2
El Yeshuatenu The God of our Salvation	Psalm 68:19
El Kanno The Jealous God	Exodus 20:5, 34:14
El Hannora The Awesome God	Nehemiah 9:32
El Shaddai The All-Sufficient God	Genesis 17:2–3

Names and Attributes of God (KJV)

Almighty	Genesis 17:1
Judge	Genesis 18:25
Eternal God	Deuteronomy 33:27
Living God	Joshua 3:10

Father of Lights	James 1:17
Lord of Hosts	1 Samuel 1:11
Fortress	2 Samuel 22:2
Lord of Lords	Deuteronomy 10:17
Heavenly Father	Matthew 6:26
Holy One of Israel	Psalm 71:22
Most High	Deuteronomy 32:8
Our Father	Matthew 6:9

Names and Attributes of the Holy Spirit (KJV)

Comforter	John 14:16
Eternal Spirit	Hebrew 9:14
Free Spirit	Psalm 51:12
Holy Spirit	Psalm 51:11; Ephesians 1:13, 4:30
Power of the Highest	Luke 1:35
Spirit of Adoption	Romans 8:15
Spirit of Burning	Isaiah 4:4
Spirit of Christ	1 Peter 1:11
Spirit of Counsel	Isaiah 11:2
Spirit of Glory	1 Peter 4:14
Spirit of God	Genesis 1:2
Spirit of Grace	Zechariah 12:10
Spirit of Holiness	Romans 1:14
Spirit of Knowledge	Isaiah 11:2
Spirit of Life	Romans 8:2
Spirit of the Lord God	Isaiah 11:2
Spirit of Might	Isaiah 11:2
Spirit of Prophecy	Revelation 19:10
Spirit of the Father	Matthew 10:20
Spirit of the Son	Galatians 4:6
Spirit of Understanding	Isaiah 11:2

Spirit of Wisdom   Isaiah 11:2
Spirit of Judgment   Isaiah 4:4

Symbols of the Holy Spirit

Dove   Matthew 3:16,17

Fire   Genesis 3:24, 22:6; 1
Kings 18:38; Acts 2:3

Oil   Exodus 30:22–31;
Psalm 23:5, 133:1–3

Rivers   Genesis 2:10; Ezekiel 47:1–5;
John 4:14, 7:38, 39

Wind   Ezekiel 37:9;Acts 2:2

Names and Attributes of Lucifer

The Bible explains human rebellion against God from several perspectives and with various images:

- doing evil: Judges 2:11
- disobedience: Romans 5:19
- transgression: Exodus 23:21; 1 Timothy 2:14
- iniquity: Leviticus 26:40
- lawlessness: Titus 2:14; 1 John 3:4
- trespass: Ephesians 2:1
- ungodliness: 1 Peter 4:18
- unrighteousness: 1 John 1:9
- unholy: 1 Timothy 1:9
- wickedness: Proverbs 11:31

Sin is always and ultimately related to God. David speaks of this:

> Against you, you only, have I sinned and
> done what is evil in your sight, so that you may
> be justified in your words and blameless in your
> judgment. (Psalm 51:4)

Sin has brought about a guilty standing before God and a corrupted condition in all humans. The pronouncement of guilt is God's legal determination that people are in an unrighteous state before him and the condition of corruption is our polluted state which inclines us toward ungodly behavior. By the grace of God, both this inherited guilt and this inherited moral pollution are atoned for by Christ:

> If we confess our sins, he is faithful and just
> to forgive us our sins and to cleanse us from all
> unrighteousness. (1 John 1:9)

Sin entered the human race in the Garden of Eden through an attack of Lucifer (a fallen angel/cherub) who led Adam and Eve to doubt God's word and trust their own ability to discern good and evil (Genesis 3). God rightly judged the rebellion of Adam and Eve and brought a curse on them and all their offspring. The curse brought physical and spiritual death, separation from God, and alienation from Him and others. All people are now conceived, born, and live in this fallen, depraved condition:

> None is righteous, no, not one; no one
> understands; no one seeks for God. All have turned
> aside; together they have become worthless; no
> one does good, not even one. (Romans 3:10–12)

> All we like sheep have gone astray; we have
> turned everyone to his own way; and the Lord has
> laid on him the iniquity of us all. (Isaiah 53:6)

Surprising as it may seem to some, Lucifer was not always evil. In the beginning, he was an angel created in perfection and beauty. Angels were given a will with a free moral choice, and Lucifer chose to do evil and rebelled against God. He was cast out of heaven to the earth because of his sin.

> How you are fallen from heaven, O shining star, son of the morning! You have been thrown down to the earth, you who destroyed the nations of the world. For you said to yourself, "I will ascend to heaven and set my throne above God's stars. I will preside on the mountain of the gods far away in the north. I will climb to the highest heavens and be like the Most High." Instead, you will be brought down to the place of the dead, down to its lowest depths. (Isaiah 14:12–15)

Lucifer had been gifted with beauty and had walked upon the holy mountain of God. But even with all this, he was not content with his position. By trying to seize God's authority, sin entered into him when he attempted to overthrow God's kingdom (Ezekiel 28:12–19). He was the first created being to exercise his freewill against God. He caused a third of the angelic beings to wage war against God (Revelation 12:4). They all have since become evil spirits due to their choice. They now roam the earth with Lucifer as their leader and master.

> Then there was war in heaven. Michael and his angels fought against the dragon and his angels. And the dragon lost the battle, and he and his angels were forced out of heaven. This great dragon—the ancient serpent called the devil, or Satan, the one deceiving the whole world— was thrown down to the earth with all his angels. Then I heard a loud voice shouting across the heavens, "It has come at last—salvation and power and

the Kingdom of our God, and the authority of his Christ. For the accuser of our brothers and sisters has been thrown down to earth— the one who accuses them before our God day and night. And they have defeated him by the blood of the Lamb and by their testimony. And they did not love their lives so much that they were afraid to die. Therefore, rejoice, O heavens! And you who live in the heavens, rejoice! But terror will come on the earth and the sea, for the devil has come down to you in great anger, knowing that he has little time." (Revelation 12:7–12)

Christians have no need to fear this evil foe as he has been defeated by Jesus Christ. He defeated him and stripped him of his power. Jesus paid the price of our sins on the cross and then rose from the dead, bringing life to all who would follow Him.

I am the living one. I died, but look—I am alive forever and ever! And I hold the keys of death and the grave (Revelation 1:18).

In this way, he disarmed the spiritual rulers and authorities. He shamed them publicly by his victory over them on the cross. (Colossians 2:15)

The Bible calls Lucifer by many names. Each name reveals a different aspect of who he is and what he does. He excels in deception, accusation, and terrifies by his roaring. He acts quick upon on opportunity to attack us with fear and hopelessness by knowing exactly our weakness. He doesn't hesitate to appeal to our pride or present us with sinful pleasure. Therefore, when you face a trial or fall into the pit of sin, do not linger in the mud, be downcast, condemned, or angry with yourself and others. Rather confess, repent, and look to the cross of Jesus Christ. Get up in His strength and rejoice, for He has won the victory over your life. Declare aloud the truth that God Almighty loves you and never will forsake you. He is always with you. Consider David when he confronted his trial with faith.

> I waited patiently for the Lord to help me, and he turned to me and heard my cry. He lifted me out of the pit of despair, out of the mud and the mire. He set my feet on solid ground and steadied me as I walked along. He has given me a new song to sing, a hymn of praise to our God. Many will see what he has done and be amazed. They will put their trust in the Lord. (Psalm 40:1–3)

Important: Meditate on the following text references before you continue:

> Text: Colossians 2:6–23, 3:1–3; Ephesians 6:10–19; James 4:7–8; 1 Peter 5:8–9; Romans 13:12; John 16:33; 2 Corinthians 10:3–5

The Names and Attributes of Lucifer (NKJV)

Abaddon (destroying Angel)	Revelation 9:11
Accuser	Revelation 12:10
Adversary	1 Peter 5:8
Angel of light (a deceiver)	2 Corinthians 11:14
Angel of the bottomless pit	Revelation 9:11
Anointed covering cherub (before his fall)	Ezekiel 28:12–14; Isaiah 14:12–14
Antichrist	1 John 4:3
Apollyon (Greek for destroyer)	Revelation 9:11
Beast	Revelation 14:9–10
Beelzebub (name of a Philistine god)	Mark 3:22; Matthew 12:24

Belial (worthless)	2 Corinthians 6:15
Deceiver	Revelation 12:9
Devil (slanderer)	1 John 3:8
Devourer	Malachi 3:11
Dragon (giant serpent)	Revelation 12:9
Enemy	Matthew 13:39
Evil one	John 17:15
Father of lies	John 8:44
God of this age	2 Corinthians 4:4
King of Babylon	Isaiah 14:4
Lawless one	2 Thessalonians 2:8–10
Leviathan (twisted sea monster)	Isaiah 27:1
Liar	John 8:44
Lucifer (shining one)	Isaiah 14:12–14
Murderer	John 8:44
Power of darkness	Colossians 1:13–14
Prince of the power of the air	Ephesians 2:1–2
Roaring lion	1 Peter 5:8
Rulers of the darkness	Ephesians 6:12
Ruler of this world	John 12:31–32
Satan	Mark 1:13
Serpent of old	Revelation 12:9
Son of perdition	2 Thessalonians 2:3–4
Tempter	Matthew 4:3
Thief	John 10:10
Wicked one	Ephesians 6:16

Time with God

Closing Thoughts Regarding the First Feast Season—Passover

Before you continue, read the story about Jesus appearing to Mary Magdalene in John 20:11–18. There is so much we can learn from Mary Magdalene. We find her deeply troubled and desperately searching for Jesus. Can we hear her hearts cry that filled every tear?

Her cry was one that showed her focus on one and one thing only—to find Jesus.

Let me ask you a question. How many times have you seen angels? Mary saw two white-robed angels that asked her, "Dear woman, why are you crying?" Notice that after she explained her heart's cry that she turned around to speak with the gardener. I personally struggle with this story.

Mary, you met and spoke with *angels…hello!* What an exceptional opportunity! Would it not be much better to find Jesus in the company of angels, rather you turned to talk with a gardener. Why? What a surprising move! However, from the story, we know that the assumed gardener was indeed Jesus Christ. Notice that she recognized Him only after Jesus spoke to her.

Are you like Mary, so single-focused on a problem that you would not let go until you find Jesus and Jesus alone? That you would not even be willing to forgo conversing with angels but rather keep searching. Your problem might be so severe that you too have not recognized Jesus at first. What a moment when everything changes while you, like Mary, hear and recognize His voice in your heart as the one you know. Mary addressed Jesus as teacher and clung to Him. In this moment of comfort, Jesus spoke to her some marvelous words. He said, "I am ascending to my Father and your Father, to my God and your God."

May the following two songs minister to you so you too can say, "*I've just seen Jesus!*" Let Jesus Christ lead you to His and your Father, to His and your God.

I've Just Seen Jesus
Daniels, William Nathan; Gather Gloria / Gather William

We knew He was dead
It is finished, He said
We had watched as His life ebbed away
Then we all stood around

Till the guards took Him down
Joseph begged for His body that day
It was late afternoon
When we got to the tomb
Wrapped his body and sealed up the grave
So I know how you feel
His death was so real
But please listen and hear what I say
I've just seen Jesus
I tell you He's alive
I've just seen Jesus
Our precious Lord alive
And I knew, He really saw me too
As if till now, I'd never lived
All that I'd done before
Won't matter anymore
I've just seen Jesus
And I'll never be the same again
It was His voice she first heard
Those kind gentle words
Asking what was her reason for tears
And I sobbed in despair
My Lord is not there
He said, Child! It is I, I am here!
I've just seen Jesus
I tell you He's alive
I've just seen Jesus
Our precious Lord alive
And I knew, He really saw me too
As if till now, I'd never lived
All that I'd done before
Won't matter anymore
I've just seen Jesus (3x)
All that I'd done before
Won't matter anymore

I've just seen Jesus
And I'll never be the same again
I've just seen Jesus!

Pass Me Not
Frances J. Crosby, 1868

Pass me not, O gentle Savior,
Hear my humble cry;
While on others Thou art calling,
Do not pass me by.
Refrain:
Savior, Savior,
Hear my humble cry,
While on others Thou are calling,
Do not pass me by.
Let me at a throne of mercy
Find a sweet relief;
Kneeling there in deep contrition,
Help my unbelief.
Trusting only in Thy merit,
Would I seek Thy face;
Heal my wounded, broken spirit,
Save me by Thy grace.
Thou the spring of all my comfort,
More than life to me,
Whom have I on earth beside Thee,
Whom in Heav'n but Thee

CHAPTER 5

THE FESTIVAL OF PENTECOST: THE SECOND FEAST SEASON

Overview:

- Fifty days after the Feast of First Fruits
- Wave offering of two loaves of leavened bread
- Promise of the Holy Spirit.
- The mystery of the church: Jews and gentiles in one body

Text: Leviticus 23:15–21; Acts 1:1–6, 2:1–47; 1 Corinthians 12:13; Ephesians 2:11–22

Tow Loaves of Leavened Bread

From the day after the Sabbath—the day you bring the bundle of grain to be lifted up as a special offering—count off seven full weeks. Keep counting until the day after the seventh Sabbath, fifty days later. Then present an offering of new grain to the Lord. From wherever you live, bring two loaves of bread to be lifted up before the Lord as a special offering. Make these loaves from four quarts of choice flour, and bake them with yeast. They will be an offering to the Lord from the first of your crops. (Leviticus 23:15–17)

This feast is also called:

- The Feast of Weeks (Exodus 34:22)
- The Feast of the Harvest (Exodus 23:16)
- The Day of the First Fruits (Numbers 28:26)
- Pentecost (Acts 2:1)

The Feast of Pentecost

The Feast of Pentecost (*Pentecost* means fifty) is observed on the fiftieth day after the Passover Sabbath. This feast lasted for one day. With the offerings on Pentecost, the Jews expressed thanksgiving, gratefulness, and dependency on God for the harvest and daily bread. The Feast of Pentecost appears to be the feast that God spoke to Pharaoh about through Moses; let my people go, so that they would hold a festival to my honor in the wilderness.

Text: Exodus 5:1, 10:9, 19:20–24

The Birthday of Judaism and Christianity

Jewish people believe that God gave the Ten Commandments to Moses on Mount Sinai on Pentecost. Therefore, Pentecost is considered the birth (day) of Judaism. Since the Holy Spirit was given on that day, Pentecost is also considered the birth (day) of Christianity.

Two Loaves of Leavened Bread

God's instructions specified offerings for the Feast of Pentecost. Among them were two loaves baked with leaven and fine flour from the wheat harvest. The priest should present these loaves as a first fruits wave offering before the Lord. These two loaves show us a remarkable prophetic sign. The fine flour used in the loaves is a symbol of Jesus. The leaven is a symbol of sin. One loaf representing the Jews, and the other the gentiles, waved before God. God accepted

both while they were still sinners. The leaven in the loaves at Pentecost speaks of the church that has not yet reached sinless perfection, even though we are filled with the Holy Spirit. In the Feast of Tabernacles, which we will learn about later, bread was made without leaven, representing a church perfected according to God's awesome plan.

Tow Loaves of Leavened Bread

Jesus Christ and the Feast of Pentecost

Jesus fulfilled the Feast of Pentecost as he was glorified and exalted to the throne of God. From there, he sent the Holy Spirit to his disciples, just as he promised.

The coming of the Holy Spirit is further proof that Jesus has been glorified as Lord. Just as the Israelites were affirmed as God's chosen people on Shavuot with the giving of the Torah, so the church was affirmed as God's chosen people at Shavuot by sending the Holy Spirit. 3000 were added to the church that day—the "first fruits" of the harvest.

Text: Acts 2; 2 Corinthians 3; Hebrews 8.

In the Jewish tradition, Shavuot is compared to a wedding, for it was on Shavuot that the covenant between God and the Jewish people was sealed on Mount Sinai. The church is called "The Bride of the messiah" and we eagerly await the marriage supper to come.

Text: Revelation 21:2,9, 19:9

After Jesus's resurrection, He appeared to His disciples on many occasions (John 20). On one such occasion, He spoke to them (John

20:22), "Receive the Holy Spirit." It is believed that the Spirit's purpose was so that they (the disciples) would be born again (be saved). In contrast, later during Pentecost when the Holy Spirit fell upon them, they were baptized in the Holy Spirit to empower them for service. After that, the disciples began to minister in the power of the Holy Spirit and in the authority of Jesus Christ. They were speaking boldly about Jesus and were witnesses to the ends of the earth.

This experience of Pentecost is the next step in our walk with Christ. The Holy Spirit is key in our lives in witnessing and ministering, in healing the broken hearted, in bringing freedom to the oppressed, and in preaching deliverance to the captives.

Text: John 20:19–22; Acts 1:4–8, 2:39; Luke 4:18–19; John 14:12; Mark 16:15–18

Time with God

What an incredible privilege and opportunity! We have become the temple of the Holy Spirit.

> Don't you realize that your body is the temple of the Holy Spirit, who lives in you and was given to you by God? You do not belong to yourself. (1 Corinthians 6:19)

At the present time, the "yeast" (sin) in the church may present many challenges. This is not so for God. God is at work in the church. God has a plan. You will find out more about this plan in the next Feast Season in which we find no "yeast." Reflect upon what is written:

> He did this to present her to himself as a glorious church without a spot or wrinkle or any other blemish. Instead, she will be holy and without fault. (Ephesians 5:27)

As for today, we find hope in what the Bible speaks about:

- The sinner:

  Well then, should we conclude that we Jews are better than others? No, not at all, for we have already shown that all people, whether Jews or Gentiles, are under the power of sin. (Romans 3:9)

  I have come to call not those who think they are righteous, but those who know they are sinners and need to repent. (Luke 5:32)

  But people are counted as righteous, not because of their work, but because of their faith in God who forgives sinners. (Romans 4:5)

  When we were utterly helpless, Christ came at just the right time and died for us sinners. But God showed his great love for us by sending Christ to die for us while we were still sinners. (Romans 5:6,8)

- The heavy burdened:

  Then Jesus said, "Come to me, all of you who are weary and carry heavy burdens, and I will give you rest. Take my yoke upon you. Let me teach you, because I am humble and gentle at heart, and you will find rest for your souls. For my yoke is easy to bear, and the burden I give you is light." (Matthew 11:28–30)

Next you find selected Bible verses and a song intended to inspire you to start your personal discovery with God, of His church and of the Holy Spirit.

That which we have seen and heard we declare to you, that you also may have fellowship with us; and truly our fellowship is with the Father and with His Son Jesus Christ ... But if we walk in the light as He is in the light, we have fellowship with one another, and the blood of Jesus Christ His Son cleanses us from all sin. (1 John 1:3,7)

Now, therefore, you are no longer strangers and foreigners, but fellow citizens with the saints and members of the household of God, having been built on the foundation of the apostles and prophets, Jesus Christ Himself being the chief cornerstone, in whom the whole building, being fitted together, grows into a holy temple in the Lord, in whom you also are being built together for a dwelling place of God in the Spirit. (Ephesians 2:19–22)

Let the word of Christ dwell in you richly in all wisdom, teaching and admonishing one another in psalms and hymns and spiritual songs, singing with grace in your hearts to the Lord. And whatever you do in word or deed, do all in the name of the Lord Jesus, giving thanks to God the Father through Him. (Colossians 3:16–17)

I will pray the Father, and He will give you another Helper, that He may abide with you forever – the Spirit of truth, whom the world cannot receive, because it neither sees Him nor knows Him; but you know him, for He dwells with you and will be in you. (John 14:16–17)

He will guide you into all truth; for He will not speak on His own authority, but whatever He hears He will speak; and He will tell you things to come. He will glorify Me, for He will take of what is Mine and declare it to you. (John 16:13–14)

If we live in the Spirit, let us also walk in the Spirit. (Galatians 5:25)

For as many as are led by the Spirit of God, these are sons of God. For you did not receive the spirit of bondage again to fear, but you received the Spirit of adoption by whom we cry out, "Abba, Father," the Spirit Himself bears witness with our spirit that we are children of God. (Romans 8:14–16)

But the fruit of the Spirit is love, joy, peace, long–suffering, kindness, goodness, faithfulness, gentleness, self–control. Against such there is no law. (Galatians 5:22–23)

The Blood Bought Church
Nancy Harmon

Verse 1
They shall lift up their voice
They shall sing for joy
They shall cry aloud and be free
They shall glorify the name of the LORD
It's the blood bought the church of the redeemed
O pick up your heart o lion of the LORD
Let the earth ring forth with his praise
All his children rejoice from the island of the sea
It's the blood bought
the church of the redeemed

Chorus
And we are in that army of the LORD
We've been washed in the blood
And we are going forth
There is nothing that could stop
This mighty moving force
With a shout of praise a two-edged sword
Every strong hold of bondage most fall
beneath our feet
Every prisoner held captive must be freed
For our deliverance has come thru
the power of the SON It's the blood bought
the church the redeemed.

Verse 2
Let earth be silent all winds cease to blow
Every created being hold your wing
For there's a new song being sung
with a new melody
It's the blood bought
the church of the redeemed.

Pentecost
Practical Guide
Introduction

The Story of Ruth

Although Pentecost (Greek) or Shavuot (Hebrew) celebrates the first fruits of the wheat harvest, other crops were ready for harvest too. From the *Talmud*, we learn that the first fruits were to be gathered when a man comes down to his field and sees a ripe fig or a perfect cluster of grapes or a beautiful pomegranate. He ties each with a red thread, saying, "These are the first fruits for the festival." In addition, the Jewish people brought two loaves of their best and finest bread for the Pentecost Festival in Jerusalem.

How to Celebrate Pentecost with Your Family

Cheese Blintzes

How about celebrating Pentecost with a festive dinner at sundown? You may make your own personal bundles of first fruit to decorate the dinner table. Take the challenge and bake two of your own special loaves of bread.

It is believed that since the story of Ruth took place against the backdrop of the barley and wheat harvest, it is connected with Shavuot. Based upon this, it became tradition to read and study the book of Ruth during this time of celebration. Keep in mind that the disciples waited for the outpouring of the Holy Spirit in the upper room until the day of Pentecost. What an opportunity you have to share these stories in your family! Include your personal experience of Pentecost and the meaning of the two-waved loaves of bread at the table.

Most agree that the traditional food for this feast is cheese, cheesecake, and especially cheese blintzes. Cheese Blintzes are thin pancakes, similar to crepes, the only difference being the incorporation of yeast into the recipe. The custom of eating dairy products on Shavuot is derived from a combination of passages of scriptures: Exodus 3:8 vocalizing the "land flowing with milk and honey;" Song of Songs 4:11 speaks about "milk and honey are under your tongue;" and Psalm 19:9–11 "the precepts of the Lord are sweeter than honey."

CHAPTER 6

ON THE ROAD TO THE PROMISED LAND

The Time in Between

This chapter gives attention to the time in between the Feast of Pentecost and Tabernacle. It is a picture when Israel spent forty years in the desert where a new generation of Jews grew up that would place their trust in God.

> You, in Your great compassion, Did not forsake them in the wilderness; The pillar of cloud did not leave them by day, To guide them on their way, nor the pillar of fire by night, to light for them the way in which they were to go. You gave Your good Spirit to instruct them, Your manna You did not withhold from their mouth, And You gave them water for their thirst. Indeed, forty years You provided for them in the wilderness and they were not in want; Their clothes did not wear out, nor did their feet swell. (Nehemiah 9:19–21)

> All the commandments that I am commanding you today you shall be careful to do, that you may live and multiply, and go in and possess the land which the Lord swore to give to your forefathers. You shall remember all the way which the Lord your God has led

you in the wilderness these forty years, that He might humble you, testing you, to know what was in your heart, whether you would keep His commandments or not. He humbled you and let you be hungry, and fed you with manna which you did not know, nor did your fathers know, that He might make you understand that man does not live by bread alone, but man lives by everything that proceeds out of the mouth of the Lord. Your clothing did not wear out on you, nor did your foot swell these forty years. Thus you are to know in your heart that the Lord your God was disciplining you just as a man disciplines his son. Therefore, you shall keep the commandments of the Lord your God, to walk in His ways and to fear Him. For the Lord your God is bringing you into a good land, a land of brooks of water, of fountains and springs, flowing forth in valleys and hills; a land of wheat and barley, of vines and fig trees and pomegranates, a land of olive oil and honey; a land where you will eat food without scarcity, in which you will not lack anything; a land whose stones are iron, and out of whose hills you can dig copper. When you have eaten and are satisfied, you shall bless the Lord your God for the good land which He has given you. (Deuteronomy 8:1–10)

And the Lord spoke to me, saying, "You have circled this mountain long enough. Now turn north." (Deuteronomy 2:2–3)

God was very close to His people in the desert. He provided for their every need. When forty years passed, God called them to enter the promised land. And yes, this time they were ready.

Is there anything Jesus pointed out that we need to do until He returns again? Is there anything connected with the forty years in the dessert? Yes, I believe so. His message carries on even beyond those forty years. Jesus gave the disciples and each believer today an invitation to abide in Him until He returns. It is the key to personal growth, authority, peace, rest, and effective ministry. We will look now at different aspects of abiding so that we too will be ready when God calls us to enter our promised land.

Abiding

At your salvation, God forgave your debt (sin) because of what Jesus Christ did for you at the cross. He procured peace between you and God. Always remember that it was by grace through faith.

> And you were dead in the trespasses and sins in which you once walked, following the course of this world, following the prince of the power of the air, the spirit that is now at work in the sons of disobedience—among whom we all once lived in the passions of our flesh, carrying out the desires of the body and the mind, and were by nature children of wrath, like the rest of mankind. But God, being rich in mercy, because of the great love with which he loved us, even when we were dead in our trespasses, made us alive together with Christ—by grace you have been saved— and raised us up with him and seated us with him in the heavenly places in Christ Jesus, so that in the coming ages he might show the immeasurable riches of his grace in kindness toward us in Christ Jesus. For by grace you have been saved through faith. And this is not your own doing; it is the gift of God, not a result of works, so that no one may boast. For we are his workmanship, created in Christ Jesus for

good works, which God prepared beforehand, that we should walk in them. (Ephesians 2:1–10)

Ponder these marvelous words of truth. You are seated with Christ in heavenly places. Continue to walk in His grace while you learn to abide in Christ. In doing so, you will discover the "Rest of God" presented in the Feast of Tabernacle. You will see the big picture of God's plan portrayed throughout the Bible.

Now I have some questions for you. Did God place in you a thirst to drink from the rivers of pleasure that are at His right hand? Do you know the longing to be free from the bondage of sin by walking pure and holy? Do you have a desire to enter your inheritance in glory and meet the Father face-to-face. Recognize that this thirst, longing, and desire are signs of God drawing us, you, to Himself. Abiding in Christ is the place where this thirst, longing, and desire is expressed by daily living with Him.

> You will make known to me the path of life;
> in your presence is fullness of joy; in your right
> hand there are pleasures forever. (Psalm 16:11)

Typically we can understand what it means to "abide by" such as rules or laws. The expression to "abide *in*" is often defined as a mystery because it is relationship oriented. Jesus Christ appeals to us that we would remain (abide) in no one other than Himself, the Son of God. It speaks of a communion that is unbroken, intimate and complete.

> Now, little children, abide in Him (*Christ
> Jesus*), so that when He (*Christ Jesus*) appears, we
> may have confidence and not shrink away from
> Him (*Christ Jesus*) in shame at His (*Christ Jesus*)
> coming. (1 John 2:28)

Clarke's Commentary on the Bible writes about this verse:

> And now, little children or beloved children,
> abide in him—in Christ Jesus. Let his word
> and spirit continually abide in you, and have
> communion with the Father and the Son.

Abiding in Christ is not achieved in one day. It takes practice and time to grow into Jesus, the Vine. Remember when you stumble and fall that you are falling only in the hands of our heavenly Father. He greatly cares for you. Watch and learn from a child that takes its first steps in life. Watch and see what happens when a child falls? At first, you may see a shocked face. Then the child will look straight up to his parents' face and laugh. With a bubbling overflow of joy and motivation to succeed, a new attempt is launched. Be like a child. Look to your father, don't hesitate to repent, get up, smile, and move on by holding on to your father's hand. There is plenty of space in the palm of God's hand for a humble heart to make mistakes.

> Though they stumble, they will never fall,
> for the Lord holds them by the hand. (Psalm
> 37:24)

Abiding in Christ will change the way you look at your day. Christians are called to have Jesus Christ as our example and be changed into His likeness; to mature and grow in Him. He walked before us, we can follow Him. Many excellent books are written on all these subjects. And there is more.

Let me illustrate this with an example. Have you ever asked yourself what Jesus would have done in your place? This seems to be a valid and normal question, particularly when you find yourself challenged by a situation and don't know how to react. Nevertheless, nowhere in the Bible do we find Jesus in a predicament wondering what to do or how His Father would react in His place. I know at first this appears to be a somewhat absurd or foolish statement. But is it not the same? What did Jesus do?

In John 5:16–29, we find the Jewish leader harassing Jesus and trying to find a way to kill him. Wouldn't you find yourself somewhat stressed in Jesus place? Listen to Jesus's words:

> So Jesus said to them, "Truly, truly, I say to you, the Son can do nothing of his own accord, but only what he sees the Father doing. For whatever the Father does, that the Son does likewise. For the Father loves the Son and shows him all that he himself is doing. And greater works than these will he show him, so that you may marvel." (John 5:19–20)

> I can do nothing on my own. I judge as God tells me. Therefore, my judgment is just, because I carry out the will of the one who sent me, not my own will. (John 5:30)

Amazing! Jesus did nothing except what He saw the Father doing or saying. So instead of asking what Jesus would have done, we need to change our focus by praying and asking the father, "Let me see what you are doing. Let me hear what you are saying." Abiding in Christ speaks of such an intimacy with the Father. It is a place where you find yourself praying and living with authority because you are stepping into the perfect will of God. Peter speaks of this place, stating it is no longer we who live, but it is Christ who lives His life through us.

> I have been crucified with Christ. It is no longer I who live, but Christ who lives in me. And the life I now live in the flesh I live by faith in the Son of God, who loved me and gave himself for me. (Galatians 2:20)

Now where do we begin to nourish such a relationship? Jesus went to a solitary place to spend time with God (Mark 1:35, NJKV). We need to do the same and learn how we can become quiet in the presence of God. Elisha recognized how a time of quiet worship effectively helped him to become quiet before God. Wait like Habakkuk and expect God will answer and speak to you.

> Be still, and know that I am God!
> (Psalm 46:10)

> "But now bring me a minstrel." And it came
> about, when the minstrel played, that the hand of
> the Lord came upon him (*Elisha*). (2 Kings 3:15)

> I will climb up to my watchtower and stand
> at my guard-post. There I will wait to see what the
> Lord says and how he will answer my complaint.
> (Habakkuk 2:1)

Let us look now on *eight different facets* on how we can nourish such an abiding relationship with God:

1. Obedience

Have you ever felt overcome by nagging guilt because you recognized your shortcomings regarding the great commission? What are some of the names that come to mind, the heroes of faith that answered Christ's call? Everyone would agree that Paul's life was exemplary in spreading the Good News about Jesus Christ. Paul's all-inspiring passion for the Lord transcends from every word of His letters. How obedient and dedicated was Paul to Christ? This question is not intended to cast a negative shadow onto Paul, rather to open our eyes to see and learn from him about abiding. Compare the two passages from Matthew and Corinthians. What do you find?

In the Book of Matthew (this passage is also known as the Great Commission):

> All authority in heaven and on earth
> has been given to me. Go therefore and make

disciples of all nations, baptizing them in the name of the Father and of the Son and of the Holy Spirit, teaching them to observe all that I have commanded you. And behold, I am with you always, to the end of the age" (Matthew 28:18–22)

In the Letter to the Corinthians:

I thank God that I baptized none of you except Crispus and Gaius, so that no one may say that you were baptized in my name. Now I did baptize also the household of Stephanas; beyond that, I do not know whether I baptized any other. (1 Corinthians 1:14–16)

At first, it appears that Paul was not obedient to the Great Commission. He states that with some exceptions, he did not baptize them. From a legal-minded point of view, that would clearly violate Christ's call to baptize. Was baptism indeed neglected? No, not at all! It was simply not carried out by him personally. Why? The next verse gives us the answer.

For Christ did not send me to baptize but to preach the gospel, and not with words of eloquent wisdom, lest the cross of Christ be emptied of its power. (1 Corinthians 1:17)

This is only one of many examples that reveal Paul's close walk with Christ. He was committed to an abiding relationship with Christ. There was no guilt or striving to perform to the world's standards and expectations of people. Nor did he question God's sovereign guidance when Christians prophesied hardship for him. His abiding obedience to Christ gave him rest in the midst of persecution.

Paul declares:

> I have been crucified with Christ. It is no
> longer I who live, but Christ who lives in me.
> And the life I now live in the flesh I live by faith in
> the Son of God, who loved me and gave himself
> for me. (Galatians 2:20)

2. Success or Failure

There is great danger in evaluating our personal growth in
Christ or even the success of our ministry through eyes dimmed by
the worlds values and standards? Let's engage in a carnal argument
about how successful Paul really was.

Imagine for a moment that you had sat next to Paul and heard
him preach. What would have been our plan of action for Paul's
continuing ministry if we would have had our saying in this matter? Naturally, we need to have him speak to thousands of people so
that the message of Jesus Christ would have been heard and spread
throughout the world. Perhaps a great evangelistic rally in one of
the Roman theaters? It seems, however, ironic, a giant mistake God
thought that the best thing would be to isolate him and place him
under house arrest. To have him guarded by Roman guards and
maybe visited by a few people. And why not have him write some
letters? What a turnaround in his life? We success-driven humans
would have a word for that—defeat or even *failure*.

It must have been absolutely devastating for Paul to be confined
in a prison. He was not able to visit the people he loved. Imagine Paul
passionately pouring out his heart when writing:

> For God is my witness, how I yearn for
> you all with the affection of Christ Jesus. And
> it is my prayer that your love may abound more
> and more, with knowledge and all discernment,
> so that you may approve what is excellent, and
> so be pure and blameless for the day of Christ,

filled with the fruit of righteousness that comes through Jesus Christ, to the glory and praise of God. (Philippians 1:8–11)

God has used Paul's letters to speak to generation after generation to millions of people. Paul would have never been able to impact so many people simply by preaching. What would the New Testament look like without God leading Paul to write his well-known letters (Ephesians, Philippians, Colossians, Philemon, and 2 Timothy) while in captivity? Today we can look back and see that the time in house arrest was indeed incredibly successful. It is you and me that can reap the fruit and blessing from Paul's hardships and struggles by letting God speak to us through his letters.

Never assume your legacy is written or is coming to an end at your death. It is God that takes the fruit of your life in His hands for His glory. Abiding has to do with listening, trusting, and obeying. It is not passive, but active, and reaches out to what has eternal value.

3. Problems or Opportunities

At times, our personal problems and life challenges may hinder us from a communion time with God. It is our human tendency to fix our eyes on our problems. The result is that the problems start dominating our lives. The Bible teaches us that we need to fix our eyes on Jesus Christ. Listen:

> Let us strip off every weight that slows us down, especially the sin that so easily trips us up. And let us run with endurance the race God has set before us. We do this by keeping our eyes on Jesus, the champion who initiates and perfects our faith. Because of the joy awaiting him, he endured the cross, disregarding its shame. Now he is seated in the place of honor beside God's throne. Think of all the hostility he endured from sinful people; then you won't become weary

and give up. After all, you have not yet given your lives in your struggle against sin. And have you forgotten the encouraging words God spoke to you as his children? He said, "My child, don't make light of the Lord's discipline, and don't give up when he corrects you. For the Lord disciplines those he loves, and he punishes each one he accepts as his child." As you endure this divine discipline, remember that God is treating you as his own children. (Hebrews 12:1–6)

There is a carnal way by which we put forth our utmost efforts by our own will power. I am speaking here about the danger of seeking the goal we pursue, and yes, even our sanctification in the power of the flesh. Great things can be achieved by the power of our will. However, it is often marked by desperate prayers of asking Jesus to bless us. This carnal way might be true only in a few situations or areas in our life—remains of dead works, the fruit of old ways of thinking and habits, ways that seemed so perfectly good. What a great testimony when Jesus explained in John 5:19, "I tell you the truth, the Son can do nothing by himself."

We are called to look to Christ alone and receive from Him by faith, step by step, day by day. Let Christ do His work in and through us by abiding in Him. Enjoying His presence and grace today will remove all doubt whether we can entrust tomorrow to Him. Only today is ours—tomorrow is the Father's.

4. Smile / Testimony (For purposes of discretion, the individuals mentioned in the following have different names)

Some time ago, sitting on a wooden chair at the kitchen table in an old county home was a young boy of about six years of age. Across the old table sat an elderly woman in her nineties eating homemade vegetable soup out of a large bowl. The boy's name was Luke, and the woman's name was Rebecca.

Luke lived a few houses down the street and was visiting Rebecca. They had been friends for quite some time. Luke was watching her quietly and slightly confused. You have to know that Luke cooked this somewhat wondrous vegetable soup. About an hour ago, he was in the garden behind the house where he found the last few vegetables—some carrots and some kind of greens.

"Yes, yes," Rebecca encouraged him. "Those greens you can eat. Bring them with you."

Luke brought the vegetables into the kitchen where he began to cut them. Soon all the vegetables were in the pot. Luke thought that there were just not enough vegetables to make a good soup. He had looked all around in the garden, hoping to find something. But nothing, nothing was left, nothing except dirt.

Then Rebecca directed him to add some water into the pot. Luke carefully placed the pot onto the old wood stove. Now he had to wait until all the vegetables became soft. On Rebecca's face was a warm smile. Indeed, with great excitement, she was looking forward to eat that soup.

Luke had generously filled up the pot with water. He hoped that by doing so, he would make more soup; it did not work. With disappointment, he watched the vegetables seemingly getting smaller and smaller the longer they were cooking. To his great surprise, it did fill up a large bowl with soup. Yes, there across the old wooden table was Rebecca eating now out of this bowl. Peace and joy were radiating from her face. Luke could just not understand.

One thing was absolutely sure and settled in his mind. There was no food anywhere in the house and certainly not in the garden. This bowl of soup was the last of her food. Rebecca would have nothing left to eat. She seemed to have no worries at all about tomorrow. She only had joy for the moment, for today.

What about tomorrow? He felt pain piercing his stomach. *Tomorrow…without food…she could get very, very hungry and maybe even…if nothing happens…die.*

"What's the matter with you, Luke? You made a wonderful delicious soup. It is warming this old body of mine and it gives me new strength," Rebecca said.

"But…but…what about tomorrow?" Luke stuttered.

"Tomorrow?" A surprised look appeared on Rebecca's face. It seemed for her a completely new thought that came from a very distant place. For a few seconds, her face became very serious. Only for a few seconds, and then like an erupting volcano, her joy and smile burst back out of her. She said, "Oh, tomorrow is in God's care. I am entrusted with today, and today is a great day. God gave me this wonderful soup and great company. You know what you do with a day that God has entrusted to you? You enjoy it and give God thanks for it. Of course, that is if you can see that He cares for you. Do you see the many wonderful and sometimes little things by which He likes to bless you? Sometimes I sing to Him to say thank you. And sometimes I have nothing left to give except a little smile. But I know He loves to see my smile."

While uttering these last words, she looked at Luke. "Do you know that He cares for you Luke?"

He lifted up his shoulders and said quietly, "I am not sure."

Seemingly changing the subject, she said, "Would you like to eat some soup? You must be hungry, take some."

Luke could barely speak. One could hardly hear him, but there it was—"No, thank you." He could not eat her last food.

Rebecca motivated him. "Luke, I can see that you are hungry. There is plenty for you and me."

"No, thanks, I'm fine," he replied. He could not eat one bit. His throat felt so tight that even if he wanted to, he could not.

After a while, Rebecca leaned back on her chair and said, "That was wonderful…mmm mmmm. You know there is some soup left. Now you can eat. I am full."

Ohhhh. How he wished that his throat would still be tight like it was before. That would make it so much easier to say no. He was so hungry. It would take all his strength to say no. Finally, he said, "You need some for dinner."

"Luke, Luke," she replied, "don't you understand? It is the now that counts. The now is significant and not the later. Now I have some left. Now I have the joy to share it with you. And now you are hungry." With that she shoved the bowl right in front of Luke.

All his willpower and all the arguments in his mind crumbled under the delicious smell of the soup. *Well*, he thought, *I can have a little bit and leave some for her, like that big carrot peeking out in the middle of the soup.*

Rebecca seemed to read his mind and said, "Dig in, there is plenty." She began to explain, "Don't you know, Luke, if God blesses you and provides for you, there is always an overflow. There is always plenty left for one more hungry mouth."

Luke could not understand how that was possible. But there he was now filled up to the brim, and there was still some soup left in the bowl. Like lightning, the thought flashed through his mind—it was enough for one more hungry mouth. "Rebecca, there is enough for your dinner…for one more hungry mouth."

Smiling but sincere, she said, "No, Luke, that doesn't count. I am not hungry. You need to find someone else."

Stunned about Rebecca's answer, Luke slowly turned his head to look around. There was no one in the house. How could he give this soup to another hungry mouth? Then he had an idea. He took the bowl of leftover soup with the spoon and charged out of the house and into the street. As soon as he reached the street, he came to an abrupt stop. Luke stood right in front of a very old man walking down the street. He almost ran into him. "Soup?" stuttered Luke and stretched out his arms with the bowl. That old man's shocked look changed into a smile.

"Sure, thank you. That is just what I need. Mmmm…vegetable soup. I love vegetable soup. That is my absolute favorite." He eagerly began spooning up the soup. Luke was standing next to him, watching him carefully. The old man seemed to enjoy every bit by making slurping noises. Abruptly, he stopped and turned the bowl upside down pouring out the rest of the soup to the ground. "That was wonderful," he said. "Thank you young man." And with that, he gave Luke back the empty bowl and left.

Startled, Luke fell to the ground, trying to pick up the last pieces of vegetables, but it was no use. They were helplessly covered in the dirt, even the one big carrot Luke recognized as the one he wanted to keep for Rebecca. She was now standing next to him. With teary eyes, Luke said, "He did not do his part to feed one hungry mouth. You know, the thing about the overflow. He just dumped the soup. He could have shared it with you. Now you will be hungry tonight."

"Luke, Luke," Rebecca said with a warm and comforting voice. "Come now. Luke, God sees your heart." She began to smile. "He sees your heart. Don't worry about the food. He sees your heart, and if you smile, he will smile back to you. Many things can happen when God smiles." She took Luke's hand and walked with him back into the house. "He sees your heart, Luke."

Weeks later, Luke found out that the vegetable soup he shared with that old man on the street was probably the last meal he had before he died a few days later. He was told that the man was known in town to be an alcoholic and had been living for a long time isolated and alone.

And what about the next day? The tomorrow? What about Rebecca? What did she have to eat the next day? Yes, Luke had visited her again. Rebecca was already sitting at the table eating some apples when Luke stepped into the kitchen. Like the day before, Rebecca smiled and was enjoying every bite. She had gotten the apples from the trees in the garden behind the house which still had some leftover fruit hanging from the harvest. They were not the prettiest looking ones. The skin was shriveled and they had some brown spots. Luke sat again on the wooden chair next to Rebecca and watched her eat. To his surprise, Rebecca sliced the whole apple, including the brown spots, and ate absolutely everything—the whole apple.

"Don't you want to cut off at least the brown spots Rebecca?" he inquired.

Now Rebecca looked surprised. "Why would I do that? Don't you eat them?"

"No, no, I always cut off the bad part from the good part," said Luke.

"But these brown spots taste like apple cider. Don't you like apple cider?" asked Rebecca with a wondrous voice.

Oh, Luke loved freshly pressed apple cider. "You think these spots taste like apple cider? I don't think so, no thank you." There is no way that he would ever try to find out if they tasted like that.

Rebecca chuckled, amused, and said quietly to herself, "Well, well, these youth nowadays. They cut off the brown spots." Luke had made her day.

Okay, how did the story go on, you may ask? What about the next day, the tomorrow? Well, I guess that is a story of God's faithfulness for another day and another book.

Today there is another all significant question waiting to be answered right at this very moment. Pause for a moment and reflect upon the story. Did you learn something of lasting value from this story? The truth is, most likely not! Surprised? That is the truth. Unless you are willing to surrender to God.

Are you willing to listen to what God has to tell you about this story? To listen and see, step by step, day by day? The question for today, for this very moment is, are you ready to abide in Him? Are you ready to answer Jesus's call? Take your time and read Luke's story again and let God surprise you. He is ready. Are you?

5. Strength or Weakness?

Within our biggest strength (talent, skill) is hidden our biggest weakness—failing! Why? Simply because we tend to be blind about the weakness that is exposed within our strength. However, if we do recognize it, our first reaction tends to be a good sounding excuse.

We need to recognize that all our strength, even the gifts we receive from God, are in need to be purified because of our tendency to defile them by sin. This crucial purification cannot be superficially produced by our own will. Otherwise, sanctification would be a matter of willpower. It would demand the necessity that Christianity is and will work only for the strong-willed. Nothing is farther from the truth.

It is said that the most fruitful heavily laden branches bow the lowest. It is all about living in a humble relationship with Jesus Christ; about me abiding in Him. There, the purification or cleansing will automatically happen by the supervision and care of a holy and loving Father, the King of Kings. Our father is the vinedresser. We are not. I invite you to replace your confidence in your own abilities with a deep confidence in the power of the Holy Spirit working in you. Don't hesitate. Act in faith what He is showing you. Surrender and yield to God. He will give you strength, joy, and rest for your soul.

> Come to Me, all who are weary and heavy-laden, and I will give you rest. Take My yoke upon you and learn from Me, for I am gentle and humble in heart, and you will find rest for your souls. For My yoke is easy and My burden is light. (Matthew 11:28–30)

What a marvelous invitation offered for the weary and heavy-laden. Experience Christ's rest as a result of being forgiven and accepted by God. The verse continues. We have to take hold of His yoke and to learn from Him. There is a necessity for the obedient to surrender. Walking humble in the path of abiding in Christ brings us to an even deeper rest, the rest of our soul.

When Jesus said, "Learn from me," He added, "I am gentle and humble in heart" to assure us that His gentleness would meet our every need. As we take steps to surrender to Him, Jesus gives us the strength and joy to do so. You will discover that it is Christ's grace, care, and strength that enables us to abide in Him. It is Jesus Christ that has taken hold of us.

> Not that I have already obtained it or have already become perfect, but I press on so that I may lay hold of that for which also I was laid hold of by Christ Jesus. (Philippians 3:12, NKJV)

> No, dear brothers and sisters, I have not achieved it, but I focus on this one thing: Forgetting the past and looking forward to what lies ahead, I press on to reach the end of the race and receive the heavenly prize for which God, through Christ Jesus, is calling us. (Philippians 3:13–14, NLT)

The New Testament defines the condition of trust, faith, and the willingness to follow and to learn from Christ as discipleship.

And there is more. May it be your prayer while you take into account

> And may the Lord cause you to increase and abound in love for one another, and for all people, just as we also do for you; so that He may establish your hearts without blame in holiness before our God and Father at the coming of our Lord Jesus with all His saints. (1 Thessalonians 3:12–13)

6. The Full Extent of Blessedness

In order that we can truly apprehend what Jesus reveals to us in John 15, we need to listen first to His teachings and prayers in John 13 and 14. Please read these two chapters before you continue.

You will quickly find out that abiding in Christ is not meant to be singled out from the rest of our faith in our Triune God. Abiding will bring you into a close relationship with God the Father, His Son, Jesus Christ, and the Holy Spirit.

> Hear, O Israel: The Lord our God, the Lord is one! (Deuteronomy 6:4)

Consider and pray about what is written in the following text regarding:

- Abide in Me (Jesus)
- Abide in My (Jesus's) love
- Abide in His (Father's) love

There is also a progression from fruit to much fruit. What brought it all about? Why is love involved to keeping His commandments?

John 15:1–17

¹I am the true vine, and my Father is the vinedresser. ²Every branch in me that does not bear fruit he takes away, and every branch that does bear fruit he prunes, that it may bear more fruit. ³Already you are clean because of the word that I have spoken to you. ⁴Abide in me, and I in you. As the branch cannot bear fruit by itself, unless it abides in the vine, neither can you, unless you abide in me. ⁵I am the vine; you are the branches. Whoever abides in me and I in him, he it is that bears much fruit, for apart from me you can do nothing. ⁶If anyone does not abide in me he is thrown away like a branch and withers; and the branches are gathered, thrown into the fire, and burned. ⁷If you abide in me, and my words abide in you, ask whatever you wish, and it will be done for you. ⁸By this my Father is glorified, that you bear much fruit and so prove to be my disciples. ⁹As the Father has loved me, so have I loved you. Abide in my love. ¹⁰If you keep my commandments, you will abide in my love, just as I have kept my Father's commandments and abide in his love. ¹¹These things I have spoken to you, that my joy may be in you, and that your joy may be full.

¹²This is my commandment, that you love one another as I have loved you. ¹³Greater love has no one than this, that someone lay down his life for his friends. ¹⁴You are my friends if you do what I command you. ¹⁵No longer do I call you servants, for the servant does not know what his master is doing; but I have called you friends, for all that I have heard from my Father I have made known to you. ¹⁶You did not choose me, but I

chose you and appointed you that you should go and bear fruit and that your fruit should abide, so that whatever you ask the Father in my name, he may give it to you. [17]These things I command you, so that you will love one another.

Jesus spoke of the cleansing of the disciples (John 13:10–11), the coming intimacy with Him and His Father (John 14:20–21,23), the coming of the Holy Spirit (John 14:16–17,26) and about love (John 13:34–35). Each of these themes (among others) is further developed in John 15, where Jesus is speaking to those who have already come to Him, and so His charge is that they remain in Him. The disciple's very life depends on this union. As branches, believers either bear fruit and are pruned to bear more fruit or they do not bear fruit and are thrown away and burned.

What is this fruit the Bible talks about in John?

The New Testament describes fruit as godly attitudes (Galatians 5:22–23), righteous behavior (Philippians 1:11), praise (Hebrew 13:15), and leading others to faith in Jesus as Messiah and Son of God (Romans 1:13–16).

So then, fruit refers to sharing in the life of God and the activities that naturally come to expression when that life is present. It is hence impossible to be united to God and at the same time remain ignorant of Him and not manifest His own characteristic love.

Jesus stresses also the impossibility of producing this fruit apart from Him. We are actually able to produce much in our own strength, without God, including converts, good deeds, and even prophesies, exorcisms, and miracles (Matthew 7:22–23). But the divine life such as we see in Jesus Christ is dependent on God's own character, power, and guidance at work in the life of the believer. Jesus did nothing; never spoke or acted for himself. Neither is the branch capable of bearing fruit "from itself." Do we understand? Are we really comprehending why Jesus commanded to remain in Him?

Jesus's disciples must make an effort to remain in the vine. Remaining is not simply believing in Him, though that is crucial but includes being in union with Him, sharing His thoughts, emotions, intentions, and power. In a relationship, both parties must be engaged. The divine must take the initiative and provide the means and the ability for the union to take place, but it cannot happen without the response of the disciple.

The verses 7–10 draw out the relationship between love and obedience (John 14:21,23–24) and views this relationship in light of the theme of mutual indwelling. Jesus dwelling in the believer is now referred to as his words remaining in them (verse 7). If they remain in Him and His words in them, Jesus promises their prayers will be answered (John 14:13–14, 15:16, 16:23–24,26). To have His words remaining in them means to share His mind and His will. They are to be caught up into the doing of God's will. Accordingly, they will pray for His purposes rather than for their own selfish desires. Jesus's purpose was to reveal God and share His life and love so people will be brought into union with Him. Such will be the concerns also of the disciples who have Jesus's words in them, and God will answer their prayers as they live according to their life in Christ and His life in them.

The other side of the mutual indwelling is the disciples remaining in Christ (verses 4,7), which is now described as the disciples remaining in His love (verse 9). Incredibly, Jesus describes this love as like the love with which His Father loved Him (John 15:9; 17:23). The Father is the source and pattern of all love, so as always, Jesus is doing that which He receives from the Father. Jesus's disciples must remain in His love (John 13:1,34; 14:21), and they do this by obeying His commands (verse 10). In part, this means they are to remain in Jesus's love for them; but more than that, it means they must remain in His own love for the Father. Jesus's own love for the Father was seen in His obeying the Father's commands and remaining in His love (verse 10). For the disciples to remain in Jesus's love for the Father, therefore, they must share in Jesus's obedience. Their obedience is itself the fruit of their remaining in Jesus because it is a characteristic of His love (1 John 2:5–6).

Jesus spoke about love and obedience that they might share in His joy (verse 11). As His word remains in them through their obedience, they are actually sharing in His life with the Father, characterized not only by obedience, but also joy. The Jewish delight in God's law (Psalm 1:2; 119:14) is here fulfilled in sharing in Jesus's own obedience to the Father.

> But they delight in the law of the Lord,
> meditating on it day and night. (Psalm 1:2)

> I have rejoiced in your laws as much as in
> riches. (Psalm 119:14)

But joy is not what comes to mind for many people when they think of obedience. Some might see obedience as conforming to rules, which portrays a demand for that person of chastising hard work. In others, it might simply kindle rebellion or hopelessness.

Rules often induce guilt in those not keeping them and a prideful delight in those who do obey. But the obedience Jesus is talking about is an obedience not to societal rules, but to the Father who is all love. To obey Him is to conform one's life to the very pattern of God's own life. Such obedience shares in His life, which is characterized by harmony, grace, goodness, and beauty. We are in intimate union with Him and swept up into His dance for which we were created and which brings the deepest fulfillment and deepest joy to our lives.

Jesus's joy came from intimacy with the Father and delight to do that which pleases the one who is all love and goodness. Jesus is showing how our joy may be complete. If we have no joy in obeying the Father, then we should consider whether we know Him as Jesus knows Him and whether we understand His will as the description of our true freedom (John 8:31–36) and joy. Indeed, we might ask ourselves what does bring us joy? The answer will reveal our own hearts.

Jesus loves just as the Father loves (verse 9), and He commands His disciples to love one another just as He loved them (verse 12). Thus, the community is characterized by divine love. If this love were just a feeling, such a command would be impossible to fulfill. But the love Jesus refers to is an act based on a certain state of heart. It is the laying down of one's life based on willing the good of the other. By God's grace we can indeed choose the good of the other, and we can choose to act accordingly. More specifically, we can choose to let Christ's pure love, that He has for the person, flow through us to the person. We can choose to see Him like Christ can see Him. This is the love Christians are called to in Christ. For Jesus says we are to love one another just as He has loved us; which He immediately defines in terms of laying down of one's life for one's friends (John 10:14–18, 13:34–35, 14:31, 15:13).

Do we recognize God's marvelous plan laid out for us in John 15? It fills me with awe and thankfulness. It is His great love, grace, and faithfulness that nourishes our hope. Join in the singing of God's praise:

Great Is Thy Faithfulness
Thomas Obediah Chisholm / William Marion Runyan

Great is Thy faithfulness!
Great is Thy faithfulness!
Morning by morning new mercies I see.
All I have needed Thy hand hath provided;
Great is Thy faithfulness, Lord, unto me!
Great is Thy faithfulness, O God my Father;
There is no shadow of turning with Thee;
Thou changest not, Thy compassions, they fail not;
As Thou hast been, Thou forever will be.
Summer and winter and springtime and harvest,
Sun, moon and stars in their courses above
Join with all nature in manifold witness
To Thy great faithfulness, mercy and love.
Pardon for sin and a peace that endureth
Thine own dear presence to cheer and to guide;
Strength for today and bright hope for tomorrow,
Blessings all mine, with ten thousand beside!

7. Being "In Christ"

By "abiding in Christ," we recognize that we are not only the temple of the Holy Spirit and that He lives in us, but we have been "placed in Christ." What does the Bible teach us about being "found in Him?" Meditate on each of the following verses. Pray and ask God for revelation concerning what it means for your life to be "in Christ." Record any insight and application that God gives you. Comments between the Bible passages are intended to provide additional thoughts to particular verses.

Romans:

3:24—being justified freely by His grace through the redemption that is in Christ Jesus.

6:11—consider yourselves to be dead to sin, but alive to God in Christ Jesus.

8:1—there is now no condemnation for those who are in Christ Jesus.

8:2—because through Christ Jesus the law of the Spirit of life set me free from the law of sin and death.

For the believer, the Spirit has replaced the law that produced only sin and death with a new simple law that produces life—the law of faith or the message of the gospel.

8:39—nor height, nor depth, nor any other created thing, will be able to separate us form the love of God, which is in Christ Jesus our Lord.

12:4–5—For as in one body we have many members, and the members do not all have the same function, so we, though many, are one body in Christ, and individually members one of another.

1 Corinthians

1:2—you who have been called by God to be his own holy people. He made you holy by means of Christ Jesus, just as he did for all people everywhere who call on the name of our Lord Jesus Christ, their Lord and ours (NLT).

1:2—to those who are sanctified in Christ Jesus, called to be saints, with all who in every place call on the name of Jesus Christ our Lord, both theirs and ours (NKJV).

1:30—by His doing, you are in Christ Jesus who became to us wisdom from God and righteousness and sanctification and redemption

By His doing, the redeemed are given a measure of His divine wisdom, imputed righteousness, sanctification from sin, and redemption by God in order that, above all else, the Lord will be glorified.

2 Corinthians

1:21—it is God who enables us, along with you, to stand firm for Christ. He has commissioned us and he has identified us as his own by placing the Holy Spirit in our hearts as the first installment that guarantees everything he has promised us.

2:14—thanks be to God who always leads us in triumph in Christ and manifests through us the sweet aroma of the knowledge of Him in every place.

2:17—we speak in Christ in the sight of God.

3:14—the veil remains "unlifted" because it is removed in Christ

The veil here represents unbelief. Those Israelites did not grasp the glory of the Old Covenant because of their unbelief. The veil of ignorance obscures the meaning of the Old Covenant to the hardened heart.

5:17—If anyone is in Christ, he is a new creature; the old things passed away; behold, new things have come.

The statement "in Christ" is of infinite significance to the believer's redemption, which includes:

- *The believer's security in Christ, who bore in His body God's judgment against sin.*
- *The believer's acceptance in Christ with whom God is well pleased.*
- *The believer's future assurance in Christ who is the resurrection to eternal life and the sole guarantor of the believer's inheritance in heaven.*
- *The believer's participation in the divine nature of Christ, the everlasting Word / see 2 Peter 1:4.*

New creation refers to the new birth. This expression includes the forgiveness of sins paid for in Christ's substitutionary death. Old value systems, priorities, beliefs, loves, and plans are gone. Evil and sin are still present, but the believer sees them in a new perspective, and they no longer control him. The believer's new spiritual perception of everything is a constant reality for him, and he now lives for eternity, not for temporal things. James identifies this transformation as the faith that produces works. See James 2:14–17; Ephesians 2:10.

5:19—God was in Christ reconciling the world to Himself, not counting their trespasses against them, and He has committed to us the word of reconciliation.

Galatians

1:22—the churches of Judea which were in Christ.

2:4—But it was because of the false brethren secretly brought in, who had sneaked in to spy out our liberty which we have in Christ Jesus, in order to bring us into bondage.

3:26—For you are all sons of God through faith in Christ Jesus

3:28—There is neither slave nor free man, there is neither male nor female; for you are all one in Christ Jesus.

Philippians

2:1–4—Therefore, if there is any consolation in Christ, if any comfort of love, if any fellowship of the Spirit, if any affection and mercy, fulfill my joy by being like-minded, having the same love, being of one accord, of one mind. Let nothing be done through selfish ambition or conceit but in lowliness of mind; let each esteem others better than himself. Let each of you look out not only for his own interests, but also for the interests of others.

Discover unity through humility.

3:14—I press on to reach the end of the race and receive the heavenly prize for which God, through Christ Jesus, is calling us.

1 Timothy

1:14—Oh, how generous and gracious our Lord was. He filled me with the faith and love that come from Christ Jesus.

2 Timothy

1:1—Paul an apostle of Christ Jesus by the will of God, according to the promise of life in Christ Jesus.

The promise of life in Christ Jesus: Those who by faith embrace the gospel's message, will be united to Christ and find eternal life in Him. See Ephesians 1:11; Romans 6:5, NLT.

1:9—who has saved us and called us with a holy calling, not according to our works, but according to His own purpose and grace which was granted us in Christ Jesus from all eternity (NASB).

For god saved us and called us to live a holy life. Not because we deserved it, but because that was his plan form before the beginning of time to show us his grace through Christ Jesus (NLT).

1:13—What you heard from me, keep as the pattern of sound teaching with faith and love in Christ Jesus.

2:1—You therefore, my son, strong in the grace that is in Christ Jesus

2:10—So I am willing to endure anything if it will bring salvation and eternal glory in Christ Jesus to those God has chosen.

2 Corinthians

1:20—For as many as are the promises of
God, in Him they are yes; therefore, also through
Him is our Amen to the glory of God through us.

*For all of God's promises have been fulfilled in Christ with a
resounding yes. And through Christ, our Amen which means yes, ascends
to God for His glory.*

*All God's Old and New Testament promises of peace, joy, love, good-
ness, forgiveness, salvation, sanctification, fellowship, hope, glorification,
and heaven are made possible and fulfilled in Jesus Christ. See Luke
24:44.*

5:21—Now He who establishes us with you
in Christ and anointed us is God.

*Christ's saving work of grace stabilizes believers and places them on
a firm foundation in Him.*

Ephesians

1:4–6—just as He chose us in Him before
the foundation of the world, that we would be
holy and blameless before Him. In love, He
predestined us to adoption as sons through
Jesus Christ to Himself, according to the kind
intention of His will, to the praise of the glory
of His grace, which He freely bestowed on us in
the Beloved.

*This is the purpose and the result of God's choosing those who are to
be saved. "In Him" refers to Christ's imputed righteousness granted to us
which places believers in a holy and blameless position before God. The
phrase "in love" belongs at the start of verse 5, by introducing the divine
motive for God's elective purpose.*

1:7—In Him, we have redemption through His Blood, the forgiveness of our trespasses, according to the riches of His grace.

1:11—Also we have obtained an inheritance, having been predestined.

1:13–14—In Him, you also, after listening to the message of truth, the gospel of your salvation—having also believed, you were sealed in Him with the Holy Spirit of promise, who is given as a pledge of our inheritance, with a view to the redemption of God's own possession, to the praise of His glory.

3:12—In whom (Christ Jesus) we have boldness and confident access through faith in Him.

Every person who comes to Christ in faith can come before God at any time; not in self-confidence, but in Christ-confidence.

Philippians

3:9—and may be found in Him, not having a righteousness of my own derived from the Law, but that which is through faith in Christ, the righteousness which comes from God on the basis of faith.

Paul's union with Christ was possible only because God imputed Christ's righteousness to him so that it was reckoned by God as his own. In Christ, there is no condemnation [Romans 8:1]. Those in Christ trust not in a legal righteousness, obtained by keeping the law, but that which is through the faith of Christ.

Colossians

1:19—For it was the Father's good pleasure for all the fullness to dwell in Him.

All the fullness, the full essence, powers, and attributes of deity dwells in Christ.

2:6–10—Therefore, as you received Christ Jesus the Lord, so walk in him, rooted and built up in him and established in the faith, just as you were taught, abounding in thanksgiving. See to it that no one takes you captive by philosophy and empty deceit according to human tradition, according to the elemental spirits of the world, and not according to Christ. For in him, the whole fullness of deity dwells bodily, and you have been filled in him who is the head of all rule and authority.

Complete in Him—believers are complete in Christ, both by position by the imputed perfect righteousness of Christ and the complete sufficiency of all heavenly resources for spiritual maturity.

1 John

1:5—God is Light, and in Him there is no darkness at all.

No darkness at all: with this phrase, John forcefully affirms that God is absolutely perfect and nothing exists in God's character that interferes with His truth and holiness.

2:5–6—But whoever keeps His word, truly the love of God is perfected in him. By this, we know that we are in Him. He who says he abides in Him ought himself also to walk just as He walked.
24:27—But the anointing which you have received from Him abides in you, and you do not need that anyone teach you; but as the same

anointing teaches you concerning all things and is true and is not a lie and just as it has been taught to you, you will abide in Him.

3:24—He who keeps His commandments abides in Him, and He in him. And by this, we know that He abides in us by the Spirit whom He has given us.

4:13—By this, we know that we abide in Him and He in us, because he has given us of his Spirit.

4:15—Whoever confesses that Jesus is the Son of God, God abides in him, and he in God.

4:16—And we have known and believed the love that God has for us. God is love, and he who abides in love abides in God, and God in him.

Colossians

2:3—In whom (Christ) are hidden all the treasures of wisdom and knowledge.

Paul declared that all the richness of truth necessary for salvation, sanctification, and glorification are found in Jesus Christ, who Himself is God revealed.

8. Statements of Truth

Now we will go one step further and specifically state some of God's blessings that belong only to the believers who are His children by faith in Christ. Declare these verses out loud! Recognize what is given to you. Let the truth set you free!

In Christ, in Him, in Whom I am…

John

✓ I am perfected in unity with God

> 17:23—I am in them and you are in me.
> May they experience such perfect unity that the
> world will know that you sent me and that you
> love them as much as you love me. (NLT)

I in them and You in Me, that they may be perfected in unity, so that the world may know that You sent Me, and loved them, even as You have loved Me. (NASB)

Ephesians

✓ I am Blessed with every spiritual blessing

> 1:3—Blessed us with every spiritual blessing
> in the heavenly places in Christ Jesus.

✓ I am chosen and adopted
✓ I am in the eternal plan of God
✓ I have a glorious future

> 1:4–5—Even before he made the world,
> God loved us and chose us in Christ to be holy
> and without fault in his eyes. God decided
> in advance to adopt us into his own family by
> bringing us to himself through Jesus Christ. This
> is what he wanted to do, and it gave him great
> pleasure.
> 3:11—This was his eternal plan, which he
> carried out through Christ Jesus our Lord

✓ I am accepted

> 1:6—To the praise of the glory of His grace, by which He made us accepted in the Beloved.

✓ I am redeemed and completely forgiven

> 1:7–10—In him we have redemption through his blood, the forgiveness of our trespasses, according to the riches of his grace, which he lavished upon us, in all wisdom and insight making known to us the mystery of his will, according to his purpose, which he set forth in Christ as a plan for the fullness of time, to unite all things in him, things in heaven and things on earth.

✓ I am given an inheritance

> 1:11—In Him also we have obtained an inheritance, having been predestined according to His purpose who works all things after the counsel of His will, to the end that we who were the first to hope in Christ would be to the praise of His glory.

✓ I am sealed and assured

> 1:13–14—In Him, you also, after listening to the message of truth, the gospel of your salvation, having also believed, you were sealed in Him with the Holy Spirit of promise, who is given as a pledge of our inheritance, with a view to the redemption of God's own possession, to the praise of His glory.

✓ I am seated with Him in heavenly places

> 2:6—raised us up with Him, and seated us with Him in the heavenly places in Christ Jesus

✓ I am brought near

> 2:13—But now in Christ Jesus you who formerly were far off have been brought near by the blood of Christ.
> 2:17–18—And He came and preached peace to you who were far away, and peace to those who were near; for through Him we both have our access in one Spirit to the Father.

✓ I am part of His church

> 2:21—We are carefully joined together in him, becoming a holy temple for the Lord. Through him you Gentiles are also being made part of this dwelling where God lives by his Spirit.

✓ I am a partaker of the promise in Christ Jesus

> 3:6—The Gentiles are fellow heirs and fellow members of the body, and fellow partakers of the promise in Christ Jesus through the gospel.

✓ I am light in the Lord

> 5:8—for you were formerly darkness, but now you are Light in the Lord; walk as children of Light.

Philippians

✓ I am called

3:13—I press on to reach the end of the race and receive the heavenly prize for which God, through (in) Christ Jesus, is calling us.

1 Corinthians

✓ I am a saint

1:2—to those who have been sanctified in Christ Jesus, saints by calling…

✓ I am enriched

1:4–5—for the grace of God which was given you in Christ Jesus, that in everything you were enriched in Him…

✓ I am made pure and holy
✓ I am freed from sin

1:30—God has united you with Christ Jesus. (by His doing you are in Christ Jesus. NASB) For our benefit God made him to be wisdom itself. Christ made us right with God; he made us pure and holy, and he freed us from sin.

✓ I am a temple for God's Spirit

6:19–20—Don't you realize that your body is the temple of the Holy Spirit, who lives in you and was given to you by God? You do not belong to yourself, for God bought you with a high price. So you must honor God with your body.

2 Corinthians

✓ I am a new creature

> 5:17—Therefore if anyone is in Christ, he is a new creature; the old things passed away; behold, new things have come.

✓ I am established, anointed and sealed

> 1:21–22—Now He who establishes us with you in Christ and anointed us is God, who also sealed us and gave us the Spirit in our hearts as a pledge—established, anointed, and sealed.

✓ I have victory
✓ I am a minister of the new covenant
✓ I am spreading out a sweet aroma

> 2:14—Now thanks be to God who always leads us in triumph in Christ, and through us diffuses the fragrance (manifests trough us the sweet aroma) of His knowledge in every place.

Romans

✓ I am free from condemnation

> 8:1—There is therefore now no condemnation to those who are in Christ Jesus, who do not walk according to the flesh, but according to the Spirit.

✓ I am secure in the love of God

> 8:38–39—But in all these things we overwhelmingly conquer through Him who loved us. For I am convinced that neither death, nor life, nor angels, nor principalities, nor things present, nor things to come, nor powers, nor height, nor depth, nor any other created thing, will be able to separate us from the love of God, which is in Christ Jesus our Lord.

Colossians

✓ I am circumcised inwardly

> 2:11–12—In Him, you were also circumcised with a circumcision made without hands, in the removal of the body of the flesh by the circumcision of Christ; having been buried with Him in baptism, in which you were also raised up with Him through faith in the working of God, who raised Him from the dead.

Philippians

✓ I am supplied with all I need

> 4:19—And my God will supply all your needs according to His riches in glory in Christ Jesus.

✓ I am rejoicing in the Lord

> 4:4–5—Rejoice in the Lord (Christ) always; again I will say, rejoice! Let your gentle spirit be known to all men. The Lord is near.

This list is by no means complete. Begin your own personal discovery for truth in the Word of God.

CHAPTER 7

INTERMEZZO II

What's Next?

It will be essential to stand back for a moment and give attention to the uniqueness of what we are about to explore in the next feast season. Up to this point, we have learned about feasts in which there is generally doctoral unity among Christians about how and when Jesus Christ fulfilled these feasts. Ahead of us, we find the feast season of Tabernacle.

You will quickly notice that not everything is so clear. Theologians, even within the same denomination, may vary considerably in its interpretation. This is in particular so regarding the time in which these events will occur in the future. There is, however, nothing to worry about. There is absolute certainty that only God's sovereign and perfect plan for the future will manifest itself in history. It will be the complete fulfillment of every stroke written in the Bible, including the book of Revelation. You may already have a preference or conviction toward one or the other of these traditional doctoral views. Let me present to you clergyman, theologian, and Biblical scholar E. W. Bullinger (1837–1913). He was a direct descendant from the influential Swiss theologian of the Protestant Reformation in the sixteenth century, J. H. Bullinger (1504–1575).

E. W. Bullinger's views were often unique and sometimes controversial. He approaches this problem of diversity in his book *Commentary on Revelation* with the following words:

> We pray God to accept and bless our humble
> effort to interpret this wonderful and important
> book. We believe He has ruled it; but where,

through any infirmity, we have misused His gifts, we pray Him to overrule it. None are more cognizant of imperfection and failure than ourselves; and, after all we have done, there is still much left for others to do. We do not exhaust the book; and may, after all, have only laid out a road on which others may follow with far greater success. We claim only one thing—an earnest desire to believe God; and to receive what He has said, regardless alike of the praise of man or the fear of man; and quite part from all traditional beliefs or interpretations.

Now let us recognize what Paul states:

> Now we see things imperfectly, like puzzling reflections in a mirror, but then we will see everything with perfect clarity. All that I know now is partial and incomplete, but then I will know everything completely, just as God now knows me completely. Three things will last forever—faith, hope, and love—and the greatest of these is love. (1 Corinthians 13:12–13)

This Intermezzo is intended to give you a short presentation about particular end-time events the Bible speaks about without favoring one view over the other. Look to God while you read each Bible verse. May God use this time to give you insight and a joyful expectation about your future, about Him, and about the Feast of Tabernacle. May you be blessed with a pure eagerness to see what God has in store for you.

The Return of Christ

The return of Jesus Christ is the central hope of the New Testament. His second coming will be sudden, personal, bodily, and visible to the whole world. He will come again to reign in power as the king of kings for all eternity. Although He has given signs that will indicate when the end times are near, God has not revealed the exact time of Christ's return.

> Text: John 14:3; Acts 1:10–11; 1 Thessalonians 4:16; Revelation 1:7; Philippians 2:9–11; Matthew 24:14, 23–29; Mark 13:10, 19–26; 2 Thessalonians 2:1–10; Matthew 24:44; Mark 13:32–33; Luke 12:40

The warnings that Christ will come unexpectedly and suddenly are intended to motivate believers to live in eager expectation and preparedness, which involves holy living with an eternal perspective. In contrast to the fear often prophesied by this world, we need to realize that the best is yet to come. On that day:

> For the Lord himself will descend from heaven with a cry of command, with the voice of an archangel, and with the sound of the trumpet of God. And the dead in Christ will rise first. Then we who are alive, who are left, will be caught up together with them in the clouds to meet the Lord in the air, and so we will always be with the Lord. Therefore, encourage one another with these words. (1 Thessalonians 4:16–18)

Christians are commanded to encourage one another with these words. Christ will return in great glory and there will be definitive, comprehensive acknowledgment that He is Lord over all. He will then judge the living and the dead. All people and forces that oppose him will be vanquished, including death itself.

> Text: Matthew 25:31; 1 Corinthians 15:24–28

The Resurrection Body

We cannot live in God's eternal heavenly glory the way we are. Our bodies have to be changed. Listen to the Apostle Paul in 1 Corinthians 15:45–58. The Scriptures tell us, "The first man, Adam, became a living person." But the last Adam—that is, Christ—is a life-giving Spirit. What comes first is the natural body, then the spiritual body comes later.

Adam, the first man, was made from the dust of the earth; while Christ, the second man, came from heaven. Earthly people are like the earthly man, and heavenly people are like the heavenly man. Just as we are now like the earthly man, we will someday be like the heavenly man.

What I am saying, dear brothers and sisters, is that our physical bodies cannot inherit the kingdom of God. These dying bodies cannot inherit what will last forever.

But let me reveal to you a wonderful secret. We will not all die, but we will all be transformed! It will happen in a moment, in the blink of an eye, when the last trumpet is blown. For when the trumpet sounds, those who have died will be raised to live forever. And we who are living will also be transformed. For our dying bodies must be transformed into bodies that will never die. Our mortal bodies must be transformed into immortal bodies.

Then when our dying bodies have been transformed into bodies that will never die, this scripture will be fulfilled:

"Death is swallowed up in victory.
O death, where is your victory?
O death, where is your sting?"
(1 Corinthians 15:54–55)

For sin is the sting that results in death, and the law gives sin its power. But thank God! He gives us victory over sin and death through our Lord Jesus Christ.

So my dear brothers and sisters, be strong and immovable. Always work enthusiastically for the Lord, for you know that nothing you do for the Lord is ever useless.

The Millennial Reign of Christ

The Book of Revelation speaks of Christ reigning for a thousand years when Satan is bound and some of God's people come to life to reign with Him (Revelation 20:1–10). Christians with evangelical roots have often interpreted this millennium in one of three ways:

- Amillennialism
- Premillennialism
- Postmillennialism

Amillennialists believe that the thousand years in Revelation 20 is figurative language showing that the reign of Christ from heaven is presently being fulfilled in the church age and will continue until the return of Christ. In this view, all the end-time events, such as Christ's return and the final judgment, happen at once.

Premillennialists believe that long before the final judgment, Christ will first return and establish his millennial kingdom; that is, His reign as king over all the earth for 1000 years. Within this view, there are various views of the timing of the great tribulation (whether Christians will go through it or will escape it by being suddenly removed from the earth before the tribulation begins) and of whether the 1000 years is a literal or a symbolic number.

Postmillennialists believe the millennial reign of Christ will be ushered in after remarkable gospel progress establishes Christ's reign on Earth, not with Christ physically present, but with the majority of the world obedient to him; and that at the end of that millennium, Christ will return in bodily form to reign over the new heavens and new earth forever.

The Final Judgment

After the millennium, Christ will judge the whole world once and for all. At this time, the righteous wrath of a Holy God will be unleashed on a rebellious world. Jesus often warned that He would usher in the day of wrath. Believers, as well as unbelievers, will be judged by Christ.

As the apostle Paul writes to the Christians at Corinth, we must all appear before the judgment seat of Christ so that each one may receive what is due for what he has done in the body, whether good or evil. The judgment of believers will test the worth of the way they lived. It will reveal that some were saved "but only as through fire."

Although God seeks to motivate his people to holy living by the rewards they will receive, ultimately, believers can stand before God only because of Christ's finished work on their behalf. The basis for justification is only the perfect righteousness imputed to believers and the diverting of sin's penalty from them to Christ and never the false security of self-righteousness. There is no fear of the final judgment for those who have trusted Christ for salvation, because there is no condemnation for those who are in Christ Jesus, which means they have confidence for the day of judgment.

Text: Isaiah 13–23; Matthew 25:31–33; 2 Timothy 4:1; 1 Corinthians 3:15, 4:5; 2 Corinthians 5:10,21; Romans 1:18–32, 2:6–11, 8:1, 14:10–12, 20:11–15; Colossians 3:23–24; Philippians 3:8–9; 1 John 4:17; Revelation 20:11–15

The New Heaven and New Earth

God's creation of the new heavens and earth is the final phase of His redeeming work. The restored creation will be freed from the tragic effects of sin and the curse, and perfect fellowship with God will be restored.

Text: Romans 8:19–23; 2 Peter 3:13

For behold, I create new heavens and a new earth, and the former things shall not be remembered or come into mind. (Isaiah 65:17)

Then I saw a new heaven and a new earth, for the old heaven and the old earth had disappeared. And the sea was also gone. And I saw the holy city, the New Jerusalem, coming down from God out of heaven like a bride beautifully dressed for her husband. I heard a loud shout from the throne, saying, "Look, God's home is now among his people! He will live with them, and they will be his people. God himself will be with them. He will wipe every tear from their eyes, and there will be no more death or sorrow or crying or pain. All these things are gone forever." (Revelation 21:1–4)

Then the angel showed me a river with the water of life, clear as crystal, flowing from the throne of God and of the Lamb. It flowed down the center of the main street. On each side of the river grew a tree of life, bearing twelve crops of fruit, with a fresh crop each month. The leaves were used for medicine to heal the nations. No longer will there be a curse upon anything. For the throne of God and of the Lamb will be there, and his servants will worship him. And they will see his face, and his name will be written on their foreheads. And there will be no night there— no need for lamps or sun—for the Lord God will shine on them. And they will reign forever and ever. (Revelation 22:1–5)

The Marriage of the Lamb

> Then I heard again what sounded like the shout of a vast crowd or the roar of mighty ocean waves or the crash of loud thunder: "Praise the Lord! For the Lord our God, the Almighty, reigns. Let us be glad and rejoice, and let us give honor to him. For the time has come for the wedding feast of the Lamb, and his bride has prepared herself. She has been given the finest of pure white linen to wear." For the fine linen represents the good deeds of God's holy people. And the angel said to me, "Write this: Blessed are those who are invited to the wedding feast of the Lamb." And he added, "These are true words that come from God." (Revelation 19:6–9)

The marriage of the Lamb has come: one reason this great multitude is so filled with praise is because the time has come for the Lamb of God to be joined with His people in a union so close it can only be compared to the marriage of a man and a woman.

The marriage of the Lamb, who is the Messiah, is a picture used frequently throughout the Scriptures. In the Old Testament, Israel is presented as God's wife who is often unfaithful (Hosea 2:19–20; Isaiah 54:5; Ezekiel 16). In the New Testament, the church is presented as the fiancé of Jesus, waiting for this day of marriage (2 Corinthians 11:2; Ephesians 5:25–32).

In Biblical times, a marriage involved two major events, the betrothal, and the wedding. These were normally separated by a period of time during which the two individuals were considered husband and wife and, as such, were under the obligations of faithfulness. The wedding began with a procession to the bride's house, which was followed by a return to the house of the groom for the marriage feast. By analogy, the church espoused to Christ by faith now awaits the *parousia* (an ancient Greek word meaning presence, arrival, or official visit); the heavenly groom will come for His bride and return to heaven for the marriage feast.

How do we make ourselves ready for this wedding? There is much for us to do, but it is ultimately a work God does in us (Ephesians 5:25–27). Paul spoke of his desire that Christians would be presented before the Lord pure:

> For I am jealous for you with godly jealousy. For I have betrothed you to one husband, that I may present you as a chaste virgin to Christ. (2 Corinthians 11:2)

Jesus Himself eagerly anticipates this marriage supper. He spoke longingly of the day when He will drink of the fruit of the vine again with His disciples in the kingdom.

Text: Matthew 26:29

CHAPTER 8

THE FESTIVAL OF TABERNACLE: THE THIRD FEAST SEASON

Overview

The Feast of Tabernacle consists of three consecutive feasts. Combined, they shape the setting of the third feast season. They symbolically show what God wants to do at the end of the age.

The Feast of Trumpets:

- Trumpet blown / a holy convocation, seventh month (Tishrei), first day
- Call for ten days of repentance (awesome days)
- Regathering of Israel in preparation for final Day of Atonement

  Text: Leviticus 23:23–25; Jeremiah 32:37–41; Ezekiel 36:24

The Feast of the Day of Atonement:

- Atonement shall be made to cleanse you, seventh month (Tishrei), tenth day
- Israel will repent and look to Messiah in one day

Text: Leviticus 16:30, 23:26–32; Zechariah 3:9–10, 12:10, 13:1–2, 14:9; Ezekiel 36:25–27; Hebrews 9,10; Romans 11:25–29

The Feast of Booths (Shelters) or Tabernacle:

- Harvest celebration/memorial of tabernacles in wilderness, seventh month (Tishrei), fifteenth day/Holy Convocation
- srael shall dwell in booths for seven days; on the eighth day, Holy Convocation
- Families of the earth will come to Jerusalem to celebrate the Feast of Booths

Text: Leviticus 23:33–44; Zechariah 14:16–19, NASB; Ezekiel 36:28

The Feast of Trumpets

The feast season of Tabernacle starts off with the Feast of Trumpets on the first day of the seventh month. It is also the Jewish New Year's Day (Rosh Hashanah) of the Jewish civil calendar. Early Jewish rabbis believed that God created the world in the first week of New Year.

> And the LORD spoke to Moses, saying, "Speak to the people of Israel, saying, In the seventh month, on the first day of the month, you shall observe a day of solemn rest, a memorial proclaimed with blast of trumpets, a holy convocation. You shall not do any ordinary work, and you shall present a food offering to the LORD." (Leviticus 23:23–25)

The Blowing of the Shofar

The Blowing of the Shofar

The feast was signified by the blowing of trumpets calling the Jews to prepare for the Day of Atonement that would be held ten days later. It gives the opportunity to repent and to be reconciled with God. These ten days of repentance were called *Yomim Noraim* which means the awesome days. Close attention is given by every Jew to search their hearts concerning repentance, reconciliation, and charitable giving. The horn that was used was the ram's horn or shofar. The ram's horn reminded the people how God provided the substitute ram sacrifice to Abraham on Isaac's behalf.

> And Abraham lifted up his eyes and looked, and behold, behind him was a ram, caught in a thicket by his horns. And Abraham went and took the ram and offered it up as a burnt offering instead of his son. So Abraham called the name of that place, "The LORD will provide"; as it is said to this day, "On the mount of the LORD it shall be provided." (Genesis 22:13–14)

We find that the horn is blown on many occasions in Israel's history. It was heard at the beginning of all feast days at the beginning of every month and at New Year. They used it when they assembled and when they moved forward on their journey. They blew the horn in warfare and to give warning.

The Feast of Trumpets in the Believer's Life

The Feast of Trumpets shows the importance of spiritual warfare in the believer's life. The closer our walk with God is, the more intense the spiritual battle gets. Our orders (jobs) for this battle are to stand in the victory Jesus won for us and to let him live through us by the power of the Holy Spirit.

In 2 Corinthians, the Bible reminds us that:

> For though we walk in the flesh, we are not waging war according to the flesh. For the weapons of our warfare are not of the flesh but have divine power to destroy strongholds. (2 Corinthians 10:3–4)

Romans 13:14 teaches us:

> Instead, clothe yourself with the presence of the Lord Jesus Christ.

Ephesians 6 specifies the armor of God. Each piece of this armor represents a critical aspect of Jesus Christ in our lives.

Let me interject with some questions at this time. Would you become a soldier to fight for a country and its people you don't know? Would you arm yourself with weapons you don't know? Would you then give your life and die for a war you don't know anything about? Besides all that, would it not be smart to train to become a soldier in the first place?

As strange as that may sound, it comes pretty close to how many approach Ephesians 6. Be aware that Ephesians starts with chapter 1 verse 1. You find greater success when you start in the beginning. Ephesians 6 will turn rich and dynamic if you know with your whole being the truth of who you are in Christ.

Become an ambassador of Christ. An ambassador knows exactly his position in Christ and the authority he has received. And most of all, an ambassador of Christ has direct access to the One he personally knows and loves. To the One that has sent him. Then Ephesians 6 will make you one of the *mighty men or women of God*.

In 2 Samuel 23:8–39, we have a list of David's heroes, also called the mighty men. This group of men were close companions and elite warriors devoted to David. You will recognize that God's hand was indeed with them. They would do extraordinary things no one else would even dare.

The men's greatness was not rooted in their own strengths or their gift for warfare. Their stories bring to light a group of men with a very deep rooted trust in God Almighty; a trust rooted by knowing they are indeed the chosen people. God was with them and fought with them in battle. With Him, they could do everything. That made them great warriors. Mighty men! These heroes of David fought war in the physical world.

I believe Ephesians prepares and equips us to become mighty men and women of God ready for battle in the spiritual world. Let's follow the teachings laid out in Ephesians and let God do His work through you. The foundation is that you are indeed placed in Christ. You are the temple of the Holy Spirit. You are crafted into the chosen people of Israel. You are made worthy and acceptable before God by the blood of Jesus Christ. Practice and abide in Christ daily. Let's blow the trumpet!

Temptation

Jesus too had his share of temptation. He was victorious by stating the truth of what is written in the word of God. Satan lost the battle completely when Jesus defeated him on the cross and sat resurrected on the right side of the throne of God Almighty. Peter says that Jesus Christ disarmed the principalities and powers and defeated the enemies of our soul. He triumphed victoriously over them.

Luke says:

> Praise be to the Lord, the God of Israel,
> because he has come and has redeemed his people.
> He has raised up a horn of salvation for us in the
> house of his servant David. (Luke 1:68–69)

Text: Luke 1:68–71; Revelation 5:12, 22–23, 19:11–16; Romans 13:14

The Feast of Trumpets and the Jewish Nation

The feasts are evidence of special encounters between God and the Jewish nation as a whole. The long summer time without any feasts until the Feast of Trumpets also speaks symbolically. The Jews rejected Jesus Christ. This period without a feast shows symbolically that God directed his favor and attention to the gentiles.

In our present time, God does not deal with Israel as a nation but on an individual basis in which the Jews too are being saved. It is, so to speak, history in the making. In the future, God will turn His attention back to the Jews as a nation, symbolized in the Feast of Tabernacles. This major encounter is signified by the return of Jesus Christ. This time, the Jews as a nation will receive Jesus Christ as their king.

Text: Revelation 1:10, 4, 5, 11:15, 19

God spoke:

> Behold, I will gather them out of all countries where I have driven them in My anger, in My fury, and in great wrath; I will bring them back to this place, and I will cause them to dwell safely. They shall be My people, and I will be their God; then I will give them one heart and one way, that they may fear Me forever, for the good of them and their children after them. And I will make an everlasting covenant with them, that I will not turn away from doing them good; but I will put My fear in their hearts so that they will not depart from Me. Yes, I will rejoice over them to do them good, and I will assuredly plant them in this land, with all My heart and with all My soul. (Jeremiah 32:37–41)

The Feast of Trumpets Ultimate Fulfillment

The ultimate fulfillment of the Feast of Trumpets is the second coming of Jesus Christ. There are many ministries today that call the church to cleansing and holiness in order to prepare the church for Jesus's second coming. Are we hearing the trumpet call seen in this feast, where the church is coming to maturity and perfection? For the great preparation for harvest ingathering and the return of the bridegroom to the bride? The church must experience the Feast of Trumpets before experiencing "the last trumpet."

Text: 1 Corinthians 15:51–57; 1 Thessalonians 4:15–18; Revelation 8–11; Matthew 25:30–31

Anticipation of Things to Come

He who has an ear, let him hear what the Spirit says to the churches. To the one who conquers I will give some of the hidden manna, and I will give him a white stone, with a new name written on the stone that no one knows except the one who receives it. (Revelation 2:17)

As God fed Israel in the wilderness, Christ supplies hidden manna to the one who conquers, who endures persecution, and stays pure from defilement (Revelation 12:6, 14–17). Historically, a white stone was given to victors at games for entrance to banquets (e.g., the messianic banquet). Such a stone was also used by jurors at trials to vote for acquittal (a judgment that a person is not guilty of the crime with which the person has been charged). The new name, given to the one who holds fast to Jesus name (Revelation 2:13), may refer to the Holy Spirit's work of conforming believers to the holiness of Christ (Romans 8:29). The manna and the white stone suggest differing types of eternal blessings and rewards.

For Christians, the call to conquer (Revelation 2:17) is sweetened by anticipation and joy of heart. They know that the time is

182

drawing near to eat and drink at the feast of all feasts, the messianic banquet. This banquet is a portrayal of the blessings of the age to come in which those chosen by God will enjoy. In the New Testament, this is often pictured as a marriage supper with Jesus Christ as the groom and the church as both bride and invited guests.

Take some time to think about what the Bible has to say about banquets.

1) The parable of the great banquet

> Luke 14:15, "Hearing this, a man sitting at the table with Jesus exclaimed, 'What a blessing it will be to attend a banquet in the Kingdom of God!'"

2) The significance of banqueting
   a) As a sign of God's goodness and mercy:

> Psalm 23:5–6, "You prepare a table before me in the presence of my enemies; you anoint my head with oil; my cup overflows. Surely goodness and mercy shall follow me all the days of my life, and I shall dwell in the house of the Lord forever" (ESV).

The mention of a table, of putting oil on the head, the cup, and the Lord's "house" all show that the psalm now describes the faithful person as God's guest at a meal (prepare a table). The enemies are powerless to prevent the enjoyment of God's generous hospitality. Goodness and mercy (or "steadfast love"/ESV footnote) are the assurance for the faithful that God has showered his grace upon them. For a non-Levite to dwell in the house of the Lord is to have ready access to the sanctuary for worship (Psalm 27:4). As the ESV footnote explains, forever is literally "for a length of days;" this may simply be another way of saying all the days of my life, but is more likely to be meant as "for days without end" (Psalm 21:4; 93:5).

b)   As a sign of fellowship with God:

Revelation 3:19–21, "I correct and discipline everyone I love. So be diligent and turn from your indifference. Look! I stand at the door and knock. If you hear my voice and open the door, I will come in, and we will share a meal together as friends. Those who are victorious (conquer) will sit with me on my throne, just as I was victorious (conquered) and sat with my Father on his throne."

Like a loving father, Christ will reprove those whom he loves (Proverbs 3:12), calling them to repent before he intervenes in judgment. To the one who opens the door, Christ will come in and eat with him—a picture of close personal fellowship.

Song of Solomon 2:4, "He escorts me to the banquet hall; it's obvious how much he loves me."

c)   As a sign to celebrating God's blessings corporately and with great joy:

Deuteronomy 16:15, "For seven days you must celebrate this festival to honor the Lord your God at the place he chooses, for it is he who blesses you with bountiful harvests and gives you success in all your work. This festival will be a time of great joy for all."

3)   The Messianic banquet as a wedding feast
a)   The invitation to participate:

Matthew 22:2, "The Kingdom of Heaven can be illustrated by the story of a king who prepared a great wedding feast for his son."

Revelation 19:7–9, "Let us be glad and rejoice, and let us give honor to him. For the time has come for the wedding feast of the Lamb, and his bride has prepared herself. She has been given the finest of pure white linen to wear. For the fine linen represents the good deeds of God's holy people. And the angel said to me, 'Write this: Blessed are those who are invited to the wedding feast of the Lamb.' And he added, 'These are true words that come from God.'"

b) The invitation rejected:

Matthew 22:3, "When the banquet was ready, he sent his servants to notify those who were invited. But they all refused to come!"

c) The invitation given to others:

Matthew 8:11–12, "And I tell you this, that many Gentiles will come from all over the world—from east and west—and sit down with Abraham, Isaac, and Jacob at the feast in the Kingdom of Heaven. But many Israelites—those for whom the Kingdom was prepared—will be thrown into outer darkness, where there will be weeping and gnashing of teeth."

4) The anticipation of the Messianic banquet
   a) It is prefigured in the Lord's Supper:

Luke 22:15–16, "Jesus said, 'I have been very eager to eat this Passover meal with you before my suffering begins. For I tell you now that I won't eat this meal again until its meaning is fulfilled in the Kingdom of God.'"

b) It is granted that you eat and drink at the table in my Kingdom:

Luke 22:29–30, "And just as my Father has granted me a Kingdom, I now grant you the right to eat and drink at my table in my Kingdom. And you will sit on thrones, judging the twelve tribes of Israel."

Rosh Hashanah
The Feast of Trumpets
Practical Guide

In the afternoon of Rosh Hashanah, the *Tashlich* is held on a nearby river or lake. "You will cast all our sins into the depths of the sea" (Micah 7:19). Each person throws a rock (or rocks) into the water to symbolize specific sins they are asking God forgiveness for.

Blow the shofar to gather everyone to the dinner table. This may be accomplished by simply playing a clip of it from the internet. The mother lights the candles and prays. There are several customary foods made for this feast. Typically, a whole fish is cooked and served by the father. An abundance of carrots is eaten as well. The backdrop for this is that the word *carrot* in Hebrew also means "to increase." Hence, that God would increase the blessings in the new year.

The bread on the table for this feast is a round shape. It serves as a symbol of hope for a full and round year. A plate full of apple slices is passed with a bowl of honey. Honey-dipped apple slices are eaten in the hope that the year will be a sweet one.

Share with the family what you learned about the Feast of Trumpets. Why is the shofar blown? The story of Abraham and Isaac from Genesis 22:1–14 is typically read after the dinner.

The Round Bread

Time with God

The Lord's Commander confronts Joshua:

> When Joshua was by Jericho, he lifted up his eyes and looked, and behold, a man was standing before him with his drawn sword in his hand. And Joshua went to him and said to him, "Are you for us, or for our adversaries?" And he said, "No; but I am the commander of the army of the LORD. Now I have come." And Joshua fell on his face to the earth and worshiped and said to him, "What does my lord say to his servant?" And the commander of the LORD's army said to Joshua, "Take off your sandals from your feet, for the place where you are standing is holy." And Joshua did so. (Joshua 5:13–15)

The sound of the trumpet is also a call to wake up. The battles of the Lord are fought on holy ground! What would have happened if Joshua had refused to take off his sandals? What could have been the consequence considering that he stood in the presence of the commander of the Lord's army with his sword drawn? Joshua did not hesitate to take off his sandals. He gave the commander divine honor. His inquiry shows an earnest desire to know the will of God and readiness to do it.

Do we display Joshua's enthusiastic readiness in our Christian walk with Christ? When are we willing to recognize that we stand on holy ground that requires (demands) that we take off our sandals (sin)? The commander's drawn sword denotes how ready he is for the defense and salvation of his people. Joshua's immediate reaction was to know whether he is friend or foe. Note that God will not take part in this conflict as an ally or adversary, but as Commander in Chief.

The wars of Israel in Canaan are always presented in the Bible as "the wars of the Lord." They were the Lord's own quarrel, and Israel and Joshua are but a division in His host. The conquest of Canaan was not a display of human cruelties (Genesis 15:16). Rather, it was a divine intervention in which human instruments were employed, but so as to be entirely subordinate to the divine will. In its core, the battle between the Israelites and Canaanites is the conflict between Christ and Beelzebub. All true Christians must fight the spiritual battle under Christ's banner, and they will conquer by His presence and their obedience to Him on holy ground.

On what ground are you standing on?

Day of Atonement

On the tenth day of the seventh month, nine days after the Feast of Trumpets, *Yom Kippur* or the Day of Atonement begins. It is the holiest day of the Jewish year. The feast provides prophetic insight regarding the second coming of the Messiah, the restoration of Israel, and the final judgment of the world.

The Day of Atonement was a day of national and sanctuary cleansing. God spoke:

> "Do no work during that entire day because it is the Day of Atonement, when offerings of purification are made for you, making you right with the Lord your God. All who do not deny

themselves that day will be cut off from God's people. And I will destroy anyone among you who does any work on that day. You must not do any work at all! This is a permanent law for you, and it must be observed from generation to generation wherever you live. This will be a Sabbath day of complete rest for you, and on that day you must deny yourselves. This day of rest will begin at sundown on the ninth day of the month and extend until sundown on the tenth day." (Leviticus 23:28–32)

Now please read God's instructions in Leviticus 19 for holiness in personal conduct.

The Holy Of Holies
Atonement By High Priest

The Torah states that Yom Kippur was the only time when the High Priest could enter the Holy of Holies and call upon the name of the Lord to offer blood sacrifice for the sins of the people. It marked the day of intercession made by the high priest on behalf of Israel.

Two goats and a bull were part of the special offerings on the Day of Atonement. The bull would be the sin offering for the high priest (Aaron) himself and his house. One of the goats was given to the Lord as sin offering. The high priest alone would enter the Holy of Holies in the temple to sprinkle the blood of the goat seven times on the Mercy Seat of the Ark. This was done to cleanse Israel from her sins, and consecrate her to God. A cloud of incense would cover the Mercy Seat.

Afterward, when the high priest would take the blood of the bull and sprinkle it seven times on the altar, the second goat or scapegoat was let go into the wilderness, carrying away the transgressions of Israel. Once a year, on the Day of Atonement, these offerings would conclude the cleansing and reconciliation with God. Atonement would be made between God and his household, the sanctuary and the nation of Israel.

The Days of Awe

In traditional Judaism, the day of Yom Kippur marks the climax of the ten-day period of repentance called the "days of awe." According to the tradition, on Rosh Hashanah, the destiny of the righteous are written in the Book of Life, and the wicked are written in the Book of Death. However, most people will not be inscribed in either book but have ten days until Yom Kippur to repent before sealing their fate. A Jew tries to amend his or her behavior and seek forgiveness for wrongs done against God and against other human beings.

The evening and day of Yom Kippur are set aside for public and private petitions and confessions of guilt. At the end of Yom Kippur, one hopes that they have been forgiven by God.

From the Rabbis Ordained Substitutes

The Jews today observe Yom Kippur as a complete fast day. There are no more atoning sacrifices possible since the destruction of the temple in Jerusalem. In place of the sin sacrifices the rabbis ordained substitutes. The substitutes are a hen or rooster slathered and given to the poor for the Yom Kippur meal, giving to charity, one's own suffering or death, the study of the Law, repentance and prayer.

The Five Afflictions

After the destruction of the temple, Rabbinic tradition stated that each individual Jew was supposed to focus on his personal service to the Lord. Most Yom Kippur prayers therefore revolve around the central theme of personal repentance. According to the Halakah, Jews must abstain from five forms of pleasures—1. eating and drinking, 2. washing and bathing, 3. applying lotions or perfume, 4. wearing leather shoes, 5. marital relations—all based on reasoning from Leviticus 23:27.

The Jews were told that they resembled angels when they fasted and prayed all day. Furthermore, by refraining from the sensual pleasures of life, they were said to have lived for twenty-five hours as if they were dead to remind them of their fate as mortals before God.

Yom Kippur Synagogue Services

Most of Yom Kippur is spent at the synagogue praying and listening to chants. It is the only Jewish holiday where tradition requires five separate distinct services for the observant Jew to attend. This day is essentially their last appeal, their last chance to change the judgment of God and to demonstrate their repentance and make compensation.

How Jesus Fulfilled the Feast of Atonement

Jesus fulfilled the Feast of Atonement by entering the heavenly holy of holies with His own blood shed on the cross for our sins. The high priest's offering in the temple needed to be repeated year after year. It only covered their sins. In the Jewish faith, there is no assurance of forgiveness of sins. Judaism is still awaiting their messiah who will bring them salvation and reconciliation with God. But Jesus Christ is the offering that cleansed us from all of our sins once and for all. We who believe in Jesus Christ as our Messiah are forgiven and made clean. To them, God declared, "I will remember your sins no more."

Judgment Before the Great White Throne

As Christian, we believe that justice was served through the sacrificial offering of Jesus Christ on the cross for our sins (2 Corinthians 5:21). Our names are written in the Lamb's Book of Life (Revelation 13:8). We are made acceptable in God's sight and not by means of our own works of righteousness (Titus 3:5–6). The Scriptures warn that on the Day of Judgment, anyone's name not found written in the Book of Life will be thrown into the lake of fire.

> Then I saw a great white throne and him who was seated on it. From his presence earth and sky fled away, and no place was found for them. And I saw the dead, great and small, standing before the throne, and books were opened. Then another book was opened, which is the book of life. And the dead were judged by what was written in the books, according to what they had done. And the sea gave up the dead who were in it, Death and Hades gave up the dead who were in them, and they were judged, each one of them, according to what they had done. Then Death and Hades were thrown into the lake of fire. This is the second death, the lake of fire. And if anyone's name was not found written in the book of life, he was thrown into the lake of fire. (Revelation 20:11–15)

The Judgment Seat of Christ

Moreover, we all will stand before the judgment seat of Christ to give account for our lives. Paul is confident that genuine believers will pass Christ's judgment, since the new covenant ministry of reconciliation has brought us under the life—the transforming power of the Spirit—based on the forgiveness of our sins through faith in Christ alone, all of which is the result of God's grace.

> So we are always of good courage. We know that while we are at home in the body we are away from the Lord, for we walk by faith, not by sight. Yes, we are of good courage, and we would rather be away from the body and at home with

the Lord. So whether we are at home or away, we make it our aim to please him. For we must all appear before the judgment seat of Christ, so that each one may receive what is due for what he has done in the body, whether good or evil (2 Corinthians 5:6–10).

Christ's Ambassador

As Christians, we need to regularly reflect on our daily lives and honestly judge our sins in the light of God. We may be in need of forgiveness and cleansing to maintain a pure relationship with God. While we are busy reflecting, it would not hurt to recognize that not only I, but we are all presently still surrounded by imperfection. Unknowingly, I may have hurt others or they may have hurt me. That challenges our calling to live by a great and overflowing generosity of forgiveness. In all of this, the apostle Paul encourages us with the following words:

Text: 1 Corinthians 10:13; 2 Corinthians 12:9–10

For God was in Christ, reconciling the world to himself, no longer counting people's sins against them. And he gave us this wonderful message of reconciliation. So we are Christ's ambassadors; God is making his appeal through us. We speak for Christ when we plead, "Come back to God!" For God made Christ, who never sinned, to be the offering for our sin, so that we could be made right with God through Christ. (2 Corinthians 5:19–21)

In our daily walk with God, the Day of Atonement teaches us how to handle trials. John the Baptist said that Jesus baptizes with the Holy Spirit and fire (John 3:16). Fire is used as a metaphor speaking of purification and cleansing. God implements these in our life by trials. The Bible speaks of these trials as a process used in purifying gold. They will test and strengthen our faith. They will build in us the character of Jesus Christ. Take assurance by knowing with confidence that we are placed on a firm foundation which is Jesus Christ. This is a knowledge that we will experience in our innermost being. Nothing can take us out of the hands of God. If we let him, God is able to turn everything into blessings.

Text: John 3:16; Job 23:8–10

The Mystery of Israel's Salvation (Romans 11)

Paul discloses in Romans 11:25–26 a mystery to the gentiles to prevent them from being proud. The word *mystery* does not necessarily refer to something puzzling or difficult to grasp, but to something that was previously hidden and is now revealed. The mystery here has three elements: (1) at this time in salvation history, the majority of Israel has been hardened; (2) during this same time, the full number of gentiles is being saved; and (3) God will do a new work in the future in which he will save all Israel.

The salvation of Israel fits with God's covenant promise to save his people and forgive their sins (Romans 11:27...when I take away their sins). The unbelief of Israel benefits the gentiles, i.e., this is the period of history in which gentiles are being saved while most of Israel remains in unbelief. But God's electing promise given to their forefathers—Abraham, Isaac, and Jacob—will be fulfilled in the future (Romans 11:28).

Salvation history is structured in Romans 11:30–31 and features God's great mercy. God saved the gentiles when one would expect only the Jews to be saved. And in the future, He will amaze us all by His grace again by saving the Jews to make it clear to all that salvation is by mercy alone. The final "now" in the text does not mean the promise to the Jews is now fulfilled but that the promise of Jewish salvation could be fulfilled at any time.

The word *all* in Romans 11:32 refers to Jews and gentiles. God's mercy is available to all, but not all will accept it. The sin and disobedience of both Jews and gentiles is highlighted to emphasize God's mercy in saving some among both Jews and gentiles.

As Paul concludes (Romans 11:33–36) his dialogue about God's great plan of salvation through history, he breaks forth into praise. Emphasized is God's wisdom and ways which are far beyond the understanding of human beings, and hence, deserving all glory. Since all things are from God, through God and for God, it follows that He deserves all the glory forever.

Text: Ezekiel 36:24–27; Hebrews 9, 10

The Second Coming of Jesus Christ

We know that God pictured His great plan of salvation in the Feast of Passover. We find Jesus's promise fulfilled about the outpouring of the Holy Spirit at the Feast of Pentecost. The feasts not only told the story of what must happen, they also had outlined the exact timeline when they would happen. Jesus's second coming is closely connected with the Feast of Tabernacle. Hence, there is a growing expectation that Jesus might return sometime during that feast. God wants us to be prepared for that great day of Christ's return. Therefore...

- Know that the one who endures tribulation to the end will be saved:

   Then they will deliver you up to tribulation and put you to death, and you will be hated by all nations for my name's sake. And then many will fall away and betray one another and hate one another. And many false prophets will arise and lead many astray. And because lawlessness will be increased, the love of many will grow cold. But the one who endures to the end will be saved. And this gospel of the kingdom will be proclaimed throughout the whole world as a testimony to all nations, and then the end will come. (Matthew 24:9–14)

- Know that it is a time of deception:

    Then if anyone says to you, "Look, here is the Christ!" or "There he is!" do not believe it. For false christs and false prophets will arise and perform great signs and wonders, so as to lead astray, if possible, even the elect. (Matthew 24:23–24)

- Know that after a loud trumpet call, angels will gather the elect:

    Immediately after the tribulation of those days the sun will be darkened, and the moon will not give its light, and the stars will fall from heaven, and the powers of the heavens will be shaken. Then will appear in heaven the sign of the Son of Man, and then all the tribes of the earth will mourn, and they will see the Son of Man coming on the clouds of heaven with power and great glory. And he will send out his angels with a loud trumpet call, and they will gather his elect from the four winds, from one end of heaven to the other. (Matthew 24:29–31)

- Know that no one knows the day or hour of Christ's return:

    But concerning that day and hour no one knows, not even the angels of heaven, nor the Son, but the Father only. (Matthew 24:36)

- Know that you must be ready for the Son of Man:

> But know this, that if the master of the house had known in what part of the night the thief was you also must be ready, for the Son of Man is coming at an hour you do not expect. (Matthew 24:43–44)

- Know that Jesus will call you to come to inherit the kingdom prepared for you:

> When the Son of Man comes in his glory, and all the angels with him, then he will sit on his glorious throne. Before him will be gathered all the nations, and he will separate people one from another as a shepherd separates the sheep from the goats. And he will place the sheep on his right, but the goats on the left. Then the King will say to those on his right, 'Come, you who are blessed by my Father, inherit the kingdom prepared for you from the foundation of the world. (Matthew 25:31–34)

- Know that the final judgment is coming:

> Then they also will answer, saying, Lord, when did we see you hungry or thirsty or a stranger or naked or sick or in prison, and did not minister to you? Then he will answer them, saying, Truly, I say to you, as you did not do it to one of the least of these, you did not do it to me. And these will go away into eternal punishment, but the righteous into eternal life. (Matthew 25:44–46)

- Know that Christ will save those (you) who are eagerly waiting for Him:

  So Christ, having been offered once to bear the sins of many, will appear a second time, not to deal with sin but to save those who are eagerly waiting for him. (Hebrews 9:28)

- Know that you can have confidence to enter the holy place:

  Therefore, brothers, since we have confidence to enter the holy places by the blood of Jesus, by the new and living way that he opened for us through the curtain, that is, through his flesh, and since we have a great priest over the house of God, let us draw near with a true heart in full assurance of faith, with our hearts sprinkled clean from an evil conscience and our bodies washed with pure water. Let us hold fast the confession of our hope without wavering, for he who promised is faithful. And let us consider how to stir up one another to love and good works, not neglecting to meet together, as is the habit of some, but encouraging one another, and all the more as you see the Day drawing near. (Hebrews 10:19–25)

- Know that you will receive what is promised:

  Therefore, do not throw away your confidence, which has a great reward. For you have need of endurance, so that when you have done the will of God you may receive what is promised. For, "Yet a little while, and the coming one will come and will not delay; but my righteous one shall live by faith, and if he shrinks back, my soul has no pleasure in him." But we are not of those who shrink back and are destroyed, but of those who have faith and preserve their souls. (Hebrews 10:35–39)

- Know that Jesus will come in the same way they saw Him go into heaven:

  And when he had said these things, as they were looking on, he was lifted up, and a cloud took him out of their sight. And while they were gazing into heaven as he went, behold, two men stood by them in white robes, and said, Men of Galilee, why do you stand looking into heaven? This Jesus, who was taken up from you into heaven, will come in the same way as you saw him go into heaven. (Acts 1:9–11)

- Know that the you will be caught up in the clouds to meet the Lord:

  For the Lord himself will descend from heaven with a cry of command, with the voice of an archangel, and with the sound of the trumpet of God. And the dead in Christ will rise first. Then we who are alive, who are left, will be caught up together with them in the clouds to meet the Lord in the air, and so we will always be with the Lord. Therefore, encourage one another with these words. (1 Thessalonians 4:16–18)

Day of Atonement
Practical Guide

The Day of Atonement or Yom Kippur fast begins an hour before sundown and lasts traditionally twenty-five hours until an hour past sundown.

> It shall be to you a Sabbath of solemn rest, and you shall afflict yourselves. On the ninth day of the month beginning at evening, from evening to evening shall you keep your Sabbath. (Leviticus 23:32)

The biggest problem with fasting is dehydration. The day before the fast, serve melon, grapes, and other foods with high water content. Avoid food and drinks with caffeine and high sugar content. Remind everyone to begin to drink plenty of water.

Before sundown and before the fast begins, a simple yet special Yom Kippur meal is eaten. Example: roasted chicken, sweet potato, baked carrots, and roasted broccoli.

This meal includes a holiday candle as well as a memorial candle at the table which is often lit in remembrance of deceased parents or grandparents. It is customary after the meal to wish everyone present an "easy fast." Another common greeting is, "May you be sealed in the Book of Life for good."

How remarkable when the entire family meets with the desire to fast. Take time to prepare so that each member of the family is ready for this day. Normally, Jewish boys under thirteen and girls under twelve fast a shorter period of time.

Kreplach

Break the fast with a simple meal such as *Kreplach*, which are dumplings filled with ground meat or mashed potatoes and served in chicken soup.

The Feast of Tabernacle

Text: Exodus 23:16

> And the LORD spoke to Moses, saying, "Speak to the people of Israel, saying, 'On the fifteenth day of this seventh month and for seven days is the Feast of Booths to the LORD. On the first day shall be a holy convocation; you shall not do any ordinary work. For seven days you shall present food offerings to the LORD. On the eighth day you shall hold a holy convocation and present a food offering to the LORD. It is a solemn assembly; you shall not do any ordinary work.'" (Leviticus 23:33–36)

> You shall keep the Feast of Booths seven days, when you have gathered in the produce from your threshing floor and your winepress. You shall rejoice in your feast, you and your son and your daughter, your male servant and your female servant, the Levite, the sojourner, the fatherless, and the widow who are within your towns. For seven days you shall keep the feast to the Lord your God at the place that the Lord will choose, because the Lord your God will bless you in all your produce and in all the work of your hands, so that you will be altogether joyful. (Deuteronomy 16:13–15)

Five days after Yom Kippur, on the fifteenth day of the seventh month, comes the Feast of Tabernacle. It is also called the Feast of Booths or Succoth (Sukkoth). For seven days, the Lord said to keep the feast. The first day and the eighth day shall be a Sabbath rest. This eighth day was a great day of rejoicing in Jerusalem.

After the harvest was gathered, the Israelites were to dwell in booths for seven days. The booths were to be built out of branches of the olive, palm, myrtle, willow, or other leafy trees. Each tree branch carried for the Israelites a symbolic meaning—the olive of anointing, the palm of victory, the myrtle of joy, and the willow of weeping.

All the Israelites and their generations to come should know that God had them live in booths when he brought them out of Egypt. They were a reminder of the first Passover in Egypt and of their disobedience which resulted in forty years of wandering in the wilderness. They should never forget that it was God who provided for them all these years. It was He that had brought them, a stiff-necked people, into the land of promise flowing with milk and honey. The booths were purposely built loosely so that the stars could be seen. It would remind the Israelites that they were pilgrims in this present life.

Since Sukkoth immediately follows the Days of Awe and repentance, it represents a time of restored fellowship with the Lord. The Tabernacle, and later the temple, represents God's presence dwelling among His redeemed people (Exodus 29:44–45). The high holidays focus on the Lord as our creator, judge, and the one who atones for our sins. The festival of Sukkoth is the time when the Jews celebrate all the Lord has done for them.

Because the Jews were commanded to rejoice for the blessing of God's provision and care in their lives during the Feast of Sukkoth (Deuteronomy 16:14–15), it is considered today especially important to give charity during this time of year.

Furthermore, it is said that King Solomon dedicated the temple during the festival of Sukkoth. (1 Kings 8:2,65)

After Israel entered the land of promise, Sukkoth was associated with the fall harvest and came to be known as the "Festival of Ingathering (of the harvest)." Certain customs were incorporated into the observance of

Lulav & Ethrog

Sukkoth, such as decorating the sukkah (shelter), performing special "wave" ceremonies (lulav), circling the synagogue in a processional while singing hymns, and reciting various Hebrew blessings to sanctify the festival.

The Lulav and Ethrog

Part of the traditional celebration and rejoicing before the Lord was the *lulav* (a closed frond of the date palm tree) or branches waved in the temple during parts of the service. Furthermore, the Jews brought the *ethrog* or citrus fruits to the temple symbolic of the bounty of the promised land that God had given them. The last harvest of the year had been successfully brought in from the fields. The land and the people were at rest. It is, so to speak, Israel's Thanksgiving festival.

Note that the Midrash (an ancient commentary on part of the Hebrew scriptures attached to the Biblical text) says that the ethrog (the citron fruit, sometimes called the "Persian Apple") was the fruit in the Garden of Eden that Adam and Eve ate in disobedience, resulting in exile from paradise. It is significant for Messianic Jews during Sukkoth to reclaim and sanctify the very means of our downfall and greatly rejoice that our sins have been atoned for through Yeshua the Messiah.

The Sukkah

The festal of Sukkoth is celebrated for seven days during which the Jews "dwell" in their huts (sukkah). During this time, they will recite various blessings, eat meals, sing songs, and wave their lulav.

> You shall dwell in booths for seven days. All native Israelites shall dwell in booths, that your generations may know that I made the people of Israel dwell in booths when I brought them out of the land of Egypt: I am the LORD your God. (Leviticus 23:42–43)

There are four kinds of organic products mentioned in the Torah regarding the festival of Sukkoth.

> And you shall take on the first day the fruit of splendid trees, branches of palm trees and boughs of leafy trees and willows of the brook, and you shall rejoice before the LORD your God seven days. (Leviticus 23:40)

Today, the Jews typically use the frond of the date palm tree (lulav), myrtle (hadass), willow (aravah) and citron (ethrog). These four items (also called "species") pertain to or are samples of the produce from the land of Israel. Some Jews like to purchase them through a Judaica merchant in order to have authentic species from the promised land. On the afternoon before Sukkoth begins, it is customary to weave the four species into a bouquet-like arrangement while standing inside your sukkah. The four items woven together are sometimes referred to as a "lulav."

The Pouring of Water

The Pouring Of Water

It was customary that the illumination of the temple and the pouring of water in the temple took place on this last day. This last day was called Hoshana Rabba which means the Day of Great Hosanna or "save now."

A priest would bring water from the Pool of Siloam to the temple in a gold pitcher. The high priest would pour this water into the basin found right by the foot of the altar as an offering. It is with this offering that the Jews prayed to God for rain. For the coming sowing season and a successful harvest, the farmers needed the rain to break the dry season. "The pouring of the water" ritual was accompanied by great celebration.

The priest would blow the trumpet, and the Jews would wave palm branches and rejoice with the singing of Psalms 113–118. The singing carried the words "save now, I pray, Lord" and "blessed is he who comes in the name of the Lord." Their prayers were directed toward God's salvation through the messiah.

Now fast forward to Jesus's time. We find the same picture by Jesus's triumphant entry into Jerusalem (Matthew 21). The Jews waved palm branches celebrating his coming. They cried out "Hosanna to the Son of David," which means, "Save us now, we pray, Son of David," and "blessed is he who comes in the name of the Lord!"

Into this "pouring of the water" celebration, we find Jesus addressing the Jews with the words found in John 7:37–39, "Anyone who is thirsty come to me." Jesus is answering their very prayers! He would give living water to anyone who believes in Him—the Holy Spirit.

The Illumination of the Temple and Jerusalem

Sunshine is also part of a successful harvest. The Jews would pray to God for the needed sunshine in the ritual of the illumination of the temple. We find also here that the Jews would pray to God for spiritual life by the messiah. The giant golden candle-

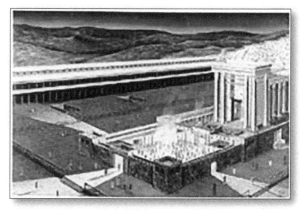

The Illumination Of The Temple

sticks in the temple would be lit. Jews from all over would bring lit torches to the temple, making so much light that both the temple and Jerusalem itself would be illuminated.

It was during the illumination of the temple that Jesus addressed the Jews with the words found in John 8:12, "I am the Light of the world!" Jesus is proclaiming that he is the light of the world. By following him, they would not be in darkness. They would have the light that would lead to life.

Simchath Torah

Torah Scroll

In the early centuries, a customary system of reading the Law was established among Jewish communities. The Law was read over a period of one year in the synagogues. The last portion of the Torah is read and celebrated on Simchath Torah by reading the blessing of Moses over the tribes of Israel. On the following Sabbath, the Jews would start reading in the beginning of Genesis. Torah translated literally means the Five Books of the Law of Moses.

Simchath Torah is a special day, set apart to rejoice over the Law or specifically "rejoicing in the Torah." On this special day of celebration, the Torah scrolls would be taken out of the ark (receptacle or ornamental closet, generally located on the wall facing Jerusalem, which contains each synagogue's Torah scrolls) and carried throughout or around the synagogue in a joyful procession seven times. Apples holding candles were placed on poles having varies decorative symbols. The children march in this parade also. Typically, they would carry flags and banners or bags with candles. Based on Psalm 19:8–10, the commandments of the Lord are sweeter than honey, so the children would be given bags of candy.

The Jewish understanding about Simchath Torah is that it cannot be celebrated at Pentecost (Shavuot), because the Torah requires our response; nor can it be celebrated on the Feast of Trumpet or on the Day of Atonement (Yom Kippur), since this represents a time of judgment and atonement. Therefore, the Jewish people wait until the end of the climactic Feast of Booths (Sukkoth) to celebrate the Torah, wherein it is said, "You will be completely joyous."

> For seven days, you shall keep the feast to the Lord your God at the place that the Lord will choose, because the Lord your God will bless you in all your produce and in all the work of your hands, so that you will be altogether joyful. (Deuteronomy 16:15)

As joyful as this celebration may appear, it misses the true joy. Isaiah speaks about it in the following words:

> All the future events in this vision are like a sealed book to them. When you give it to those who can read, they will say, We can't read it because it is sealed." When you give it to those who cannot read, they will say, "We don't know how to read." And so the Lord says, "These people say they are mine. They honor me with their lips, but their hearts are far from me. And their worship of me is nothing but man–made rules learned by rote. Because of this, I will once again astound these hypocrites with amazing wonders. The wisdom of the wise will pass away, and the intelligence of the intelligent will disappear. (Isaiah 29:11–14)

The Jewish people are still waiting until Jesus will fulfill and open their eyes, when the seal will be broken, and their vision undimmed. On this day of fulfillment, the Jews will recognize Jesus Christ as the messiah. This day will then be a true Simchath Torah celebration of joy.

Jesus and the Feast of Tabernacles

Jesus Christ made it possible. In Him and through Him, we can tabernacle with God. In Jesus, we experience the dwelling place and fullness of God. There is a rest found in His presence. The book of Hebrews reminds us that we must enter this rest. In order to be able to enjoy God's rest here on Earth, we have to walk with Him in loving trust and obedience (abide in Him).

Hebrews 3:7, "Today when you hear his voice, don't harden your hearts as Israel did when they rebelled."

The Israelites failed to enter God's rest. Their rebellious hearts resulted in forty years of wilderness. What a special blessing for the soul that God has awaiting for those found in Jesus at Tabernacle until we will enter our heavenly rest.

The final completion of the Feast of Tabernacle is revealed in the Book of Revelation chapter 21. John saw a new heaven and a new earth. The old had passed away. The New Jerusalem is coming down out of heaven. A voice from the throne of God said in Revelation 21:3, "Behold, the tabernacle of God is with men, and he will dwell with them, and they shall be his people." God Himself will be with them and be their God.

Zion—Jerusalem

In the "Intermezzo," we already touched on different traditional views concerning the end-time events. Now I want to direct our attention to a Messianic Jewish view that awaits fulfillment in the Festival of Sukkoth. Note that God has not forgotten His holy city Jerusalem and His chosen people.

Here the "Day of Ingathering" of the harvest, Sukkoth, prefigures the gathering together of the Jewish people in the days of the Messiah's reign on earth.

> Yet the time will come when the Lord will
> gather them together like handpicked grain. One
> by one he will gather them—from the Euphrates

River in the east to the Brook of Egypt in the west. In that day the great trumpet will sound. Many who were dying in exile in Assyria and Egypt will return to Jerusalem to worship the Lord on his holy mountain. (Isaiah 27:12–13)

"In that day," says the Lord, "when people are taking an oath, they will no longer say, 'As surely as the Lord lives, who rescued the people of Israel from the land of Egypt.' Instead, they will say, 'As surely as the Lord lives, who brought the people of Israel back to their own land from the land of the north and from all the countries to which he had exiled them.' Then they will live in their own land." (Jeremiah 23:7–8)

All of the nations of the earth that survive the Great Tribulation will come together to worship the Lord in Jerusalem during the Feast of Sukkoth.

In the end, the enemies of Jerusalem who survive the plague will go up to Jerusalem each year to worship the King, the Lord of heaven's Armies, and to celebrate the Festival of Shelters. Any nation in the world that refuses to come to Jerusalem to worship the King, the Lord of heaven's Armies, will have no rain. (Zechariah 14:16–17)

This view of Sukkoth also foreshadows the Lord's sheltering presence over Israel in the millennial kingdom. No longer will Israel be subject to the oppression of the ungodly nations of the world, but God Himself will place His sanctuary in her midst.

And I will make a covenant of peace with them, an everlasting covenant. I will give them their land and increase their numbers, and I will put my Temple among them forever. I will make my home among them. I will be their God, and they will be my people. And when my Temple is among them forever, the nations will know that I am the Lord, who makes Israel holy" (Ezekiel 37:26–28)

We know that Yeshua, our messiah, did indeed come to "sukkah" or "tabernacle" with us in order to purge our sins and redeem us to Himself.

So the Word became human and made his home among us. He was full of unfailing love and faithfulness. And we have seen his glory, the glory of the Father's one and only Son. (John 1:14)

With eyes of faith, we see the glory of the divine presence of the Lord God Almighty in the person of Yeshua, our beloved and holy anointed one. With eagerness, we await His return to establish His kingdom and "tabernacle with us" again. At that time, Yeshua will set up His everlasting Sukkah, so that we may know, love, and abide with Him forever.

Time With God

Freedom

Sukkoth reminds us that slavery to our old sinful life is not an option for the redeemed people of the Lord. God wants us to be free from the bondage of our past. We must leave behind our old identities and dependencies on anything other than God Himself; that is, brought forth and refined in the wilderness experience of faith.

God calls us to walk in the presence of His love, not in the fear of man. We are a new creation in the Messiah, reborn to take possession of the promises God has given to us. Our citizenship is in heaven from which also we eagerly wait for a savior, Jesus Christ, Yeshua, the Messiah, our Lord who will transform the body of our humiliation to be like His glorious body according to the working of His power that enables Him to subject all things to Himself (Philippians 3:20–21).

What an incredibly awesome time that lies ahead of us when we meet Jesus Christ, our savior. May the joy of the Lord overshadow you while you join in the singing and rejoicing of these two songs.

Days of Elijah
Mark Robin

These are the days of Elijah
Declaring the word of the Lord.
And these are the days of Your servant Moses
Righteousness being restored
These are the days of great trials
Of famine and darkness and sword
Still we are the voice in the desert crying
Prepare ye the way of the Lord!
Say, behold He comes, riding on the clouds
Shining like the sun at the trumpet's call
Lift your voice, year of Jubilee
Out of Zion's hill, salvation comes.
And these are the days of Ezekiel
The dry bones becoming flesh
And these are the days of Your servant, David
Rebuilding a temple of praise
And these are the days of the harvest
The fields are all white in Your world
And we are the laborers that are in Your vineyard
Declaring the Word of the Lord
Say, behold He comes, riding on the clouds
Shining like the sun at the trumpet's call
Lift your voice, year of Jubilee

Out of Zion's hill, salvation comes
Behold He comes, riding on the clouds
Shining like the sun at the trumpet's call
Lift your voice, year of Jubilee
Out of Zion's hill, salvation comes
There's no God like Jehovah!
(12x)

Behold He comes, riding on the clouds
Shining like the sun at the trumpet's call
Lift your voice, year of Jubilee
Out of Zion's hill, salvation comes
Behold He comes, riding on the clouds
Shining like the sun at the trumpet's call
Lift your voice, year of Jubilee
Out of Zion's hill, salvation comes.

Jerusalem
Alpert Herb

John saw a city that could not be hidden
John saw the city, oh yes he did
John caught a glimpse of the golden throne
Tell me all about it, go right on
Around the throne he saw the crystal sea
There's got to be more, what will it be
I want to go, to that city he saw
New Jerusalem
Jerusalem
I want to walk your streets that are golden
And I want to run where the angels have trod
Jerusalem
I want to rest on the banks of your river
In that city, the city of God
John saw the lion lay down by the lamb

I want to know everything about that land
John saw the day but he did not see night
The lamb of God well, he must be the light
And he saw the saints worship the great I am
Crying worthy, worthy is the lamb
I want to go to that city he saw
New Jerusalem
Jerusalem, Jerusalem
Sing for the night is over
Hosanna in the highest
Hosanna forever
Forever more
Jerusalem
I want to walk your streets that are golden
And I want to run where the angels have trod
Jerusalem
I want to rest on the banks of your river
In that city, the city of God
The city of God
Jerusalem, Jerusalem
The city of God, is the city of God

The Feast of Tabernacles Practical Guide

This is a great opportunity to build a hut (shelter/sukkah) with your family. Use some branches to loosely cover the roof and sides of your hut. The huts are small and hastily built. Since the sukkah is intended to serve as your "home" for the next eight days, it is customary to decorate it with palm branches, flowers, fruit, or vegetables, etc. Make sure that you are able to see the stars through the roof at night. You may even enjoy eating your Tabernacle dinner in your hut.

The children will love to sleep in the hut and listen to the story of Tabernacle. A sukkah may be built in a yard, on a flat roof, or even on a balcony. Those who live in apartments or in locations where it is impossible to build a sukkah often help their congregation or another family decorate their sukkah during this time.

The Jews rejoice over the law at Tabernacle by having a Torah procession. How much more reason do we have to rejoice over having the Word of God, the Bible. We too can have a procession in our home or around our house. Sing some praise songs with your children as you march with your Bible in hand.

Unlike other holidays, Sukkoth has no traditional foods other than kreplach. Any dish incorporating the harvest of one's own region is appropriate for Sukkoth.

CHAPTER 9

THE FEASTS OF THE JEWS
These Feasts Were Not Commanded by God

Overview

- The Feast of Hanukkah
- The Feast of Purim
- The Ceremony of Bat Mitzvah & Bar Mitzvah

The Feast of Hanukkah (Chanukkah)

Text: John 10:22–23

Hanukkah is also called The Feast of Dedication or The Feast of the Lights. Hanukkah is not rooted in the Feasts of the Lord found in the Old Testament. The historical backdrop of Hanukkah reaches back to Alexander the Great. Motivated by his vision of one Greek culture, he Hellenized the people under his rule. Antiochus Epiphanes was a Syrian king that came to power from 175–163 BC. He was one of the successors of the now divided kingdom of Alexander the Great. By cruel enforcement of Greek culture onto the people of Israel, Epiphanes tried to end the Jewish religion. He was successful to an extent in doing so among the more liberal and free-thinking sections of the priesthood.

Antiochus Epiphanes plundered and defiled the temple. To show his disrespect to the God of the Jews, he sacrificed a pig to Jupiter on the altar. Mattathias the Maccabee, head of a priestly family together with a remnant core of Jews, refused to abandon their faith. The Maccabean revolt eventually gained the Jewish people their independence.

Judas Maccabees cleansed the temple from all defilement that took place under the rule of Antiochus. He removed the defiled altar and placed its stones into a hidden corner of the temple. He restored the worship of the Lord and all the cleansing came to an end on the twenty-fifth day of Kislev (December), 164 BC.

The rededication of the temple lasted for eight days. It was a great and joyous celebration in which they sang the Hallel daily. It is said that the Maccabean Jews found a small jar of consecrated oil. This small jar of oil would only supply light in the temple for one night. It miraculously lasted for eight days. After that, new oil was ready, prepared, and consecrated. It was decreed that candles shall be lit in memory of this wonderful rededication, God's miraculous provision, and God freeing them out of the hand of their enemy.

The Talmud and Hanukkah

Interestingly, the story of Hanukkah derives from the Apocrypha (1 Maccabees 4:52–59), except that there is no mention of the oil nor of the miracle of the oil. Only until we reach the later part of the *Talmud*, a commentary on the *Mishnah* completed around 500 AD, do we hear anything about the miracle of the oil in connection with the rededication of the temple. Regardless of the mystery in the origin of Hanukkah, Rabbinic tradition has instituted various rules and customs for the observance of this eight-day festival to commemorate the Jews victory over their enemies. Among these are:

- Celebrating Hanukkah for eight days from Kislev 25 to Tevet 3 on the Jewish calendar (*Talmud*: Shabbat 21b).
- The nightly kindling of the menorah was designed to recall the miracle of the eight days in which the sanctified oil burned in the temple. With the menorah's increasingly brighter light, it is a symbol of Godly resistance to both tyranny and the forces of assimilation (*Talmud*: Sukkah 46a).

- Be joyous on Hanukkah and avoid signs of sadness (*Talmud*: Shabbat 21b).

The Nine-Branched Menorah

Hanukkah is a Feast of God's faithfulness and deliverance. Each evening as the sun sets, Jewish families light a candle on the nine-branched menorah. The ninth candle serves as the servant candle to light the rest—one candle for each day until on the eighth day the menorah is fully lit. On the first night, the first candle (or oil) is lit on the right side of the menorah. On each night thereafter, the leftmost candle is lit first and continues from left to right. The candle should burn for at least one half hour after it gets dark. Typically, three blessings are recited during the eight days of the festival. They are usually said before or after the candles are lit. It is customary in many Jewish homes to sing Hanukkah songs after the lighting of the candles. Some also recite Psalms such as 30, 67, and 91.

Nine-Branched Menorah

The last night of Hanukkah is called *Zot Chanukah* (this is Hanukkah). It remembers the dedication of the altar (Numbers 7:84). It marks the grand finale of the Hanukkah celebration when the supernatural light burns brightest.

Note: On Shabbat (Friday night), you light the Hanukkah candles before lighting the Shabbat candles.

It is an old custom to display the Hanukkah menorah where its lights will be visible from the outside. If you place the Hanukkah menorah near a window, the candles should appear lit right to left from the point of view of those seeing them from the outside. Many families have multiple Hanukkah menorahs, one for each child of the family and perhaps a larger one for the entire family.

Three Traditional Hanukkah Blessings

1) Blessing over the candles

Barukh atah Adonai, Eloheinu, melekh halo's asher kidishanu b'mitz'votav v'tzivanu l'had'lik neir shel Chanukkah. Amein.

Translation:
Blessed are you, Lord, our God, sovereign of the universe Who has sanctified us with His commandments and commanded us to light the lights of Hanukkah. Amen.

2) Blessing for the Hanukkah

Barukh atah Adonai, Eloheinu, melekh halo's she'asah nisim la'avoteinu bayamim haheim baziman hazeh. Amein.

Translation:
Blessed are you, Lord, our God, sovereign of the universe Who performed miracles for our ancestors in those days at this time. Amen.

3) Shehecheyanu (who has given us life) blessing (first night only)

Barukh atah Adonai, Eloheinu, melekh halo's shehecheyanu v'kiyimanu v'higi'anu laz'man hazeh. Amein.

Translation:
Blessed are you, Lord, our God, sovereign of the universe who has kept us alive, sustained us, and enabled us to reach this season. Amen.

Hanukkah Songs

Maoz Tzur—O Mighty Stronghold
(The following is a literal translation from a classic Hanukkah song)

O mighty stronghold of my salvation,
to praise You is a delight.
Restore my House of Prayer
and there we will bring a thanksgiving offering.
When You will have prepared the slaughter
for the blaspheming foe,
Then I shall complete with a song of hymn
the dedication of the Altar.
My soul had been sated with troubles,
my strength has been consumed with grief.
They had embittered my life with hardship,
with the calf–like kingdom's bondage.
But with His great power
He brought forth the treasured ones,
Pharaoh's army and all his offspring
Went down like a stone into the deep.
To the holy abode of His Word He brought me.
But there, too, I had no rest
And an oppressor came and exiled me.
For I had served aliens, and had drunk benumb-
ing wine.
Scarcely had I departed
At Babylon's end Zerubabel came.
At the end of seventy years I was saved.
To sever the towering cypress
sought the Aggagite, son of Hammedatha,
But it became (a snare and) a stumbling block
to him
and his arrogance was stilled.

The head of the Benjaminite You lifted
and the enemy, his name You obliterated
His numerous progeny – his possessions –
on the gallows You hanged.
Greeks gathered against me
then in Hasmonean days.
They breached the walls of my towers
and they defiled all the oils;
And from the one remnant of the flasks
a miracle was wrought for the roses.
Men of insight—eight days
established for song and jubilation
Bare Your holy arm
and hasten the End for salvation—
Avenge the vengeance of Your servants' blood
from the wicked nation.
For the triumph is too long delayed for us,
and there is no end to days of evil,
Repel the Red One in the nethermost shadow
and establish for us the seven shepherds.

Rock of Ages
Marcus Gastric and Gustav Gottheil
(Popular paraphrased English version)

Rock of Ages, let our song
Praise Thy saving power;
Thou, amidst the raging foes,
Wast our sheltering tower.
Furious they assailed us,
But Thine arm availed us,
And Thy Word
Broke their sword
When our own strength failed us.

Kindling new the holy lamps,
Priests, approved in suffering,
Purified the nation's shrine,
Brought to God their offering.
And His courts surrounding
Hear, in joy abounding,
Happy throngs,
Singing songs
With a mighty sounding.
Children of the martyr race,
Whether free or fettered,
Wake the echoes of the songs
Where ye may be scattered.
Yours the message cheering
That the time is nearing
Which will see
All men free,
Tyrants disappearing.

I Have a Little Dreidel
(Traditional children's Hanukkah song)

I have a little dreidel
I made it out of clay
And when it's dry and ready
Then dreidel I shall play!
O dreidel, dreidel, dreidel
I made it out of clay
And when it's dry and ready
Then dreidel I shall play!
It has lovely body
With legs so short and thin
And when my dreidel's tired
It drops and then I win!

My dreidel's always playful
It loves to dance and spin
Oh happy game of dreidel
Come play now, let's begin!

Hanukkah Traditions

Hanukkah is not an additional Sabbath holiday, therefore there is no obligation to refrain from or any activities which are forbidden on a Sabbath. Work and school is going on as usual, but it is normal to leave in time to be home to kindle the lights at nightfall. The exception is in Israel were schools are closed from the second day to the end of Hanukkah. It is customary for many families to exchange small gifts each night.

Fried foods are eaten to commemorate the miracle when a small flask of oil kept the flame in the temple alight for eight days. Traditional foods include potato pancakes, known as "latkes," jam-filled doughnuts, and *bimuelos* or a fried dough ball.

Fried Dough Ball   Doughnuts   Potato Pancakes

Dreidel

The dreidel is a four-sided top that children play with on Hanukkah after the lighting of the Menorah candle. It has one Hebrew letter on each side.

Dreidel

For dreidels used in Israel:

נ (Nun), ג (Gimmel), ה (Hay) and פ (Pey), which stand for the Hebrew phrase "Nes Gadol Haya Po." This means "A great miracle happened here."

Outside of Israel, those letters are:

נ (Nun), ג (Gimmel), ה (Hay) and ש (Shin), which stand for the Hebrew phrase "Nes Gadol Haya Sham." This phrase means "A great miracle happened there (in Israel)."

How to Play the Dreidel Game

Any number of people can play the dreidel game. At the beginning of the game, each player is given an equal number of *gelt* (coin) pieces or candy, usually ten to fifteen.

At the beginning of each round, every player puts one piece into the center "pot." They then take turns spinning the dreidel with the following meanings assigned to each of the Hebrew letters:

> **INSIGHT**
>
> Yiddish is a high German language of Ashkenazi Jewish origin spoken in many parts of the world. It developed as a fusion of Hebrew and Aramaic into German dialects with the infusion of Slavic and traces of romance languages. It is written in Hebrew alphabet.

- *Nun* means "nichts," which means "nothing" in Yiddish. If the dreidel lands on nun, the spinner does nothing.
- *Gimmel* means "ganz," which is Yiddish for "everything." If the dreidel lands on gimmel, the spinner gets everything in the pot.
- *Hey* means "halb," which means "half" in Yiddish. If the dreidel lands on hey, the spinner gets half of the pot.
- *Shin* means "shtel," which is Yiddish for "put in." *Pey* means "pay." If the dreidel lands on either a shin or a pey, the player adds a coin to the pot.

If a player runs out of game pieces, they are "out."

Jesus and the Feast of Hanukkah

In John 10:22, we learn that Jesus was in Jerusalem at the time of Hanukkah, the Festival of Dedication.

> It was now winter, and Jesus was in Jerusalem at the time of Hanukkah, the Festival of Dedication. He was in the temple, walking through the section known as Solomon's Colonnade. The people surrounded him and asked, "How long are you going to keep us in suspense? If you are the Messiah, tell us plainly." Jesus replied, "I have already told you, and you don't believe me. The proof is the work I do in my Father's name. But you don't believe me because you are not my sheep. My sheep listen to my voice; I know them, and they follow me. I give them eternal life, and they will never perish. No one can snatch them away from me, for my Father has given them to me, and he is more powerful than anyone else. No one can snatch them from the Father's hand. The Father and I are one. (John 10:22–30)

Historically, the Maccabean revolt and rule happen in the time between the Old and New Testament. Therefore, a reference to the festival of Hanukkah occurs in the New Testament and not in the Tanakh (canon of the Hebrew Bible). In this season of remembering miracles, Jesus Christ pointed out that the works that He did attested to His claim to be the long awaited messiah of the Jewish people. His works and character clearly displayed the true light of who He was, and these works still shine to us today.

Jesus commanded us:

You are the salt of the earth, but if salt has lost its taste, how shall its saltiness be restored? It is no longer good for anything except to be thrown out and trampled under people's feet. You are the light of the world. A city set on a hill cannot be hidden. Nor do people light a lamp and put it under a basket, but on a stand, and it gives light to all in the house. In the same way, let your light shine before others, so that they may see your good works and give glory to your Father who is in heaven. (Matthew 5:13–16)

Jesus told us:

I am the light of the world. Whoever follows me will not walk in darkness, but will have the light of life. (John 8:12)

We are called to be part of His temple, His body. Reflect on these thoughts and dedicate yourself to be free from the compromise that tempts us to assimilate ourselves with the evil bound world around us. It's only by the light of Jesus Christ that we gain victory over the powers of darkness, since the darkness cannot comprehend the light.

Let us walk in the light:

This is the message we have heard from him and proclaim to you, that God is light, and in him is no

---

INSIGHT

Interesting math:

The Bible doesn't give us an exact date for Jesus birth. The early Christians believed that The Feast of Dedication points to the day Jesus was born. Others concluded that Hanukkah was the time when Jesus was conceived. Jesus is the light that came into this world. He is the ninth candle by whom all others are lit.

This conclusion is drawn upon that in Luke 1:5, we learn that Zechariah was a member of the priestly order of Abijah. Rabbinic writings show that the division of Abijah served as priests during the second half of the fourth month of the Jewish religious calendar.

Elisabeth conceived John the Baptist late June. She was six months pregnant when she saw Mary to tell her the good news (Luke 1:24–26). This calculation would have Jesus conceived sometime in the month of December and born nine months later at Succoth when the Word of God became flesh and tabernacled among us (Luke 1:5, 24–26).

darkness at all. If we say we have fellowship with him while we walk in darkness, we lie and do not practice the truth. But if we walk in the light, as he is in the light, we have fellowship with one another, and the blood of Jesus his Son cleanses us from all sin. If we say we have no sin, we deceive ourselves, and the truth is not in us. If we confess our sins, he is faithful and just to forgive us our sins and to cleanse us from all unrighteousness. If we say we have not sinned, we make him a liar, and his word is not in us. (1 John 1:5–10)

May we behold the glory of His light by abiding in His love! And may we turn to Him now and rededicate our own lives as temples cleansed and filled by His spirit to honor His abiding presence.

The Feast of Purim
The History of Purim

(Queen Esther)

In Ezra 1, we read that God fulfilled the prophecy he had given through Jeremiah. God stirred the heart of King Cyrus of Persia to build God a temple at Jerusalem (538 B.C.). The king allowed any who are his people (Jews) to go to Jerusalem to rebuild this temple of the Lord God of Israel. Not all of the Jews followed King Cyrus' call.

The events unfolding into the Feast of Purim are written in the book of Esther and happened in the days of King Xerxes who reigned over Persia from 486–465 BC. His kingdom had 127 provinces and stretched from India to Ethiopia. He ruled the Persian Empire from his royal throne at the fortress of Susa (Esther 1:1–4). Two of the Jews remaining in exile and living in Susa were Esther and Mordecai.

The Persian Empire

Mordecai offended Haman, the royal vizier, and told King Ahasuerus, so Haman's fury burned not only against Mordecai but against all the Jews. He decided the exact day on he would attack the Jews by casting a lot. The Feast of Purim comes from the word *pur*, which translates to "lots." The lot Haman cast fell upon the thirteenth day of Adar. That is why this feast is called Purim.

Queen Esther came before the king and exposed Haman's evil plot. The king issued a decree and it was written exactly as Mordecai dictated, causing Haman's plot to backfire. The king's decree gave the Jews in every city authority to unite to defend their lives (Esther 8: 1–13).

Haman and Mordecai

It would be interesting to know why Mordecai and Esther remained part of the diaspora in Susa, as opposed to returning to Jerusalem. Unfortunately, the Bible gives us no reason. In Esther 2:21, Mordecai was sitting at the king's gate, probably as an official because of Esther's influence with the king. Part of Persian court etiquette was to bow to superiors. It was not seen as on act of worship. The reason for Mordecai's refusal to bow is stated as "he was a Jew." It appears that Mordecai could not bow without compromising his identity as a Jew. There is a possibility that Haman was claiming some kind of divine status as did the Persian kings. As a faithful Jew,

Mordecai would not give him that honor. Fascinating is the family line of these two men.

Caution is also placed here as to not come to faulty conclusions. Mordecai is identified as being from Benjamin, descendant of Saul (Esther 2:5). Haman the Agagite is possibly related to the Amalekites. This would mean that the genesis of Haman (Esther 3:1) reaches back to the time when the Jews exited from Egypt and were attacked by the Amalekites (Exodus 17:14), whose lineage began with Amalek, grandson of Esau (Genesis 36:12). Saul received orders to kill all the Amalekites. He disobeyed God by refusing to kill King Agag. Samuel finally killed Agag with the sword (1 Samuel 15:32–33). It is reasonable to think that even 550 years after king Agag's death, these two men would know of their tribal hostility. This could also be a possible explanation why Mordecai refused to bow down to Haman whose ancestors had attempted to exterminate the Jewish people before. Whatever the reason, by his refusal, Mordecai gave Haman the opportunity to destroy the Jews in the whole kingdom of Ahasuerus, which included Jerusalem and the surrounding area with its mainly Jewish population (Esther 3:5–6).

The Feast of Purim commemorates the Jewish people living in the Persian Empire being saved from extermination. It is celebrated on the fourteenth and fifteenth day of Adar. In Esther 9:20–22, we read how the Feast of Purim is to be celebrated. Mordecai recorded all these events and sent letters to the Jews near and far throughout all the provinces of King Xerxes, calling on them to celebrate an annual festival on these two days. He told them to celebrate these days with feasting and gladness and by giving gifts of food to each other and presents to the poor. This would commemorate a time when the Jews gained relief from their enemies when their sorrow was turned into gladness and their mourning into joy.

Observing Purim Today

Purim, like Hanukkah, is a joyous festival which has no religious laws attached by the Torah. Jewish people observe these days "as days of feasting and gladness." There are Purim parades held in which children and adults alike dress up. You may meet Queen Esther, Mordecai, or see any of the known figures of the story.

A special prayer called the *Amidah* (the standing prayer) is resided in the evening, morning, and afternoon as well as in the prayer of grace after meals. The Amidah is also called the *Shmoneh Esreh* (the Eighteen) in reference to the original number of constituent blessings that are the central prayer of the Jewish liturgy. This prayer, among others, is found in the traditional Jewish prayer book called *Siddur*.

Jews are held to four main *mitzvoth* (obligations) to fulfill at Purim. The *FIRST* one is to listen to the public reading of the Book of Esther. This is usually observed in the synagogue. Never should they forget what happened so long ago. When Haman's name is read (which occurs fifty-four times), the congregation engages in noise-making to blot out his name. In contrast, the listeners cheer at the heroes in the story.

SECOND is the mitzvah of sending (not personally, but by a messenger or third party) Purim baskets (gift baskets of food and drinks) to friends, family, and neighbors. It is meant to ensure that everyone has enough food for the Purim feast held later in the day and to increase love and friendship among Jews as a counter to Haman's assertion that the Jewish people are characterized by strife and disunity. Typically, these Purim food baskets are filled with treats such as challah bread, chocolates, wine, dried fruits, a variety of nuts, and other ready to eat gourmet foods. It is said that Purim is not truly celebrated without *hamentashen*, which are delicious triangle-shaped cookies that symbolize Haman. There can be found in a wide range of flavors such as raspberry, chocolate, prune, poppy seed, or apricot.

THIRD, Purim includes giving at least two Purim gifts of food to those less fortunate. These are also traditionally sent as gift baskets, but the mitzvah can also be fulfilled by a financial contribution to an organization that will ultimately provide food.

The last and *FOURTH* mitzvah is fulfilled by eating a festive meal together at the closing of the Purim celebration. There is no traditional Purim menu. Nevertheless, kreplach, and for dessert, hamentashen, are highly popular among the Jews for this joyous meal, customarily served with wine.

Hamentashen

A Perfect Picture of Jesus Christ

Similar to the story in the book of Esther, all of us who have sinned have been issued a decree of death. Through the intervention of Jesus Christ, the old decree has been satisfied and a new proclamation of eternal life has been established. Therefore, the deliverance by the working of Mordecai is a perfect picture of Jesus our Messiah. Haman visualizes Lucifer with his accusations and plans to kill. The new decree issued to save the Jews points to the new covenant. Now through Jesus Christ, our sorrows are indeed turned into gladness and our mourning into joy.

Bat Mitzvah & Bar Mitzvah Ceremony
Introduction

- *Bar Mitzvah* literally translates as "son of commandment." The word *bar* means "son" in Aramaic. The word *mitzvah* is Hebrew for "commandment."
- *Bat Mitzvah* literally translates as "daughter of commandment." The word *bat* means "daughter" in Aramaic.

The term *Bar* or *Bat Mitzvah* refers to two things: It is used to describe a boy (thirteen years of age) or girl (twelve years of age) when they "come of age." It also refers to the religious ceremony in Jewish communities that accompanies a boy or girl becoming a Bar Mitzvah or Bat Mitzvah. Often a party will follow the ceremony, which is also called a Bar or Bat Mitzvah.

> **INSIGHT**
>
> Aramaic was the "everyday" language of the Jewish people and much of the Middle East from around 500 BC to 400 AD.

It is important to note that the ceremony and celebration are not required by Jewish custom. Rather, a Jewish boy will automatically become a Bar Mitzvah at age thirteen. The specifics of the ceremony and the following party will vary widely depending on which movement the family is a member of (Orthodox, Reform, etc.). In a traditional family, the appropriate date for a bar or bat mitzvah is the Shabbat on or following the child's birthday.

History

The term *Bar Mitzvah* in the sense it is now used cannot be clearly traced back earlier than the fourteenth century. The modern method of celebrating becoming a Bar Mitzvah did not exist at the time of the Bible. What we do know is that passages in the books of Exodus and Numbers note the age of majority for military service as twenty. The term Bar Mitzvah appears first in the *Talmud* compiled in the early first millennium. The age of thirteen is also mentioned in the *Mishnah* as the time one is obligated to observe the Torah's commandments. It states that at the age of five, a person should study the scriptures; at ten, the *Mishnah*; and at thirteen, the commandments.

Nevertheless, some speculate that the roots of the Bar Mitzvah go back to the day of the second temple period. It was said that a Bar Mitzvah boy would be brought to the temple courtyard to receive the priests and elders blessings. We can only speculate if perhaps the New Testament accounts of the twelve-year-old Jesus in the temple were included to show us that He passed through the traditional Jewish rites of His day. Whether or not Jesus actually became Bar Mitzvah, we know that His relationship to the written Law was perfect in every way.

Understanding the Tradition of Bar/Bat Mitzvah

How relevant is Bar or Bat Mitzvah today for a Jewish believer in Jesus Christ? Is there perhaps something Christian's can learn from it? There are plenty of opinions in the messianic Jewish community regarding this event. All rally around the question whether a Jewish Christian should maintain the practice of Bar Mitzvah. This is not to be mistaken with the fact upon which all Messianic Jews agree that our relationship with God is based solely on our faith in Jesus Christ. The burden of the law has been lifted at Calvary.

Let's dig deeper. God gave the commandments to the Israelites through Moses. A Jewish parent rejoices by calling their child a son or daughter of the commandment. Bar Mitzvah celebrates the Torah by seeing it handed down from generation to generation. In doing so, God's Word has a central role in the service. This ceremony testifies of God's promise that He has chosen to preserve His people.

Bar/Bat Mitzvah is also a sign to the child that he or she is a Jew. While the children grow up, their sense of identity grows too. The children take the necessary steps to become Bar Mitzvah while they are taught about their faith and begin to obtain ownership of their Jewish identity. They learn by observing their parents and others in the synagogue. They begin striving to attain what is of great value to them. The children will learn to understand what it means to be a Jew and to live as a Jew by participating in the customs that express the Jewish culture. The Bar Mitzvah ceremony therefore expresses a lifecycle event which is very significant to the Jewish family. It presents a wonderful way of bringing a family closer together and communicates to family and friends the value of a common heritage.

A thirteen-year-old is likely to feel too old to be a child but too awkward, inexperienced, and dependent to be an adult. You may recall your personal challenges at this age. Were you obedient in following God, regardless of the pressure you felt to "follow the crowd?" In times like this, one's faith becomes one's own. Accountability is an important aspect of maturity. It is helpful to have a landmark event, a "rite of passage," to memorialize the fact that young adults must take responsibility for their actions.

Traditionally, the Bar Mitzvah declares a young person's coming to their own to family and friends. While not totally abandoned and left to their own at thirteen years old, being Bar Mitzvah gives them a foundation of scripture and relationship with God to face challenging situations. Bar Mitzvah contributes to the understanding of spiritual responsibility and obligation. Boys and girls need and deserve respect before they are thirteen, but this "coming of age" gives them the opportunity to present themselves as responsible members of the community. The Bar Mitzvah ceremony is the Jewish time to recognize that a child is growing up.

While you read this, you may be tempted to think of baptism. Remember, Bar Mitzvah speaks of identifying with the Jewish people and heritage, while baptism speaks of identifying with Jesus Christ.

It has become the custom in many synagogues for the Torah to be passed from grandparents to parents to the Bar/Bat Mitzvah (young adult), symbolizing the passing down of the obligation to engage in the study of Torah and Judaism.

While the Bar/Bat Mitzvah ceremony is a milestone event and is the culmination of years of study, it is not the end of a boy or girl's Jewish education. It marks the beginning and commitment of a lifetime of Jewish learning, study, and participation in the Jewish community.

Don't Miss the Opportunity in Your Family

I believe that the tradition of Bar or Bat Mitzvah can present great opportunities for any Christian parent. Bar/Bat Mitzvah recognizes the significant role both parents have in teaching their children about their faith and heritage. This preparation to the day of the child's Bar/Bat Mitzvah is not primarily seen as a classroom style teaching (although the teaching of a Rabbi is often part of this preparation); rather it is a natural learning by which the parents live out their faith at home while the child grows up. It is a real and close up practical leaning experience.

Furthermore, up to the age of twelve or thirteen (the day of Bar/Bat Mitzvah), children usually have a very tender and open spirit to learn and receive from us parents. Dad's especially have to recognize how precious that trust is that your child places in you. Your child believes everything you say in a simple "childlike" way. You may be tempted to misuse that trust and make jokes about and with it. Stop it! Don't abuse it.

> Fathers, do not provoke your children to anger by the way you treat them. Rather, bring them up with the discipline and instruction that comes from the Lord (Ephesians 6:4).

A child usually builds his or her first impression of God by seeing and interacting with his or her dad at a very young age. What a marvelous privilege dads have to use the trust and love of a child to point to our heavenly Father.

Celebrating the Feasts of Israel by revealing Jesus Christ in them is a wonderful opportunity for your child to learn about your faith in Jesus Christ and heritage in Him. As they grow, our hope is that they will learn to make our faith their own.

What more can we do in our home that embraces the idea of preparing our children "to come of age?" How about the idea of having a few minutes of family devotion time at your breakfast table? How about reading one Bible verse, singing one verse of a hymn or song, and saying a short prayer before your start to eat? You might sing first while you sit together at the table. Obviously you can begin this tradition when the child is an infant. Then your child can grow up with the understanding that this is the way to start the day. The morning gathering is a succession, not a law. In some families, it will be much easier to rally together in the evening for a devotion, perhaps after dinner, or in the quietness of an ending of the day. Do what will work best in your family.

Another tremendous opportunity given to you is reading the Bible through with your children (a good starting age is about six) and studying the word of God from cover to cover. You may want to take advantage of a year's Bible which has sections of Old and New Testament, Psalms and Proverbs written for every day the year. In the beginning, divide one day reading into two or more days, otherwise it will be too much for them. Don't be in a rush. This is not a performance race. It may take you several years to finish. In other words, the process toward the goal and the enjoyment of it is far more important than actually reaching the goal.

Be sensitive to the guidance of the Holy Spirit. Expect that He will be present to guide and speak to all. A vital part of this regular gathering is to listen to each child. What is the child telling you about what is read? The Psalms and Proverbs give plenty of wisdom to talk about where God's values and wisdom can be embraced in daily living. During the history portion of the Bible, you may discuss questions like this: What do you think God will do next? How will He react? Such questions will nurture our insight about God and His love, grace, and mercy.

Think about the awesome privilege given us in that he has chosen us to worship Him. You may have some songs that are very close to your heart, songs that have moved your spirit. These songs are special to you and express your love, thankfulness, and praise to God. Sing them with your children while they are still small and eager to learn. Consider also teaching your child some hymns. Tell them about the great stories that motivated these people to write these hymns which are so rich in text. You can find books today in the market that tell these stories along with each hymn.

Needless to say, parents have plenty of opportunities to teach their children before they reach their twelfth or thirteenth birthday. Be creative. Pray about it. Let God guide you. Every family will be different in how that can and will work out.

Bar / Bat Berakhah

Who do you think is closer to God's heart? Parents that roll their eyes with a hopeless expression when their child reaches the teenage years? Or parents that recognize the privilege and authority given them by welcoming the child into this stage of life? We want a child who is prepared and blessed by his parents; one that takes responsibility for his actions. And we mark the occasion with a celebration that recognizes this "becoming of age" or the "right of passage" from childhood to adulthood. This can be a day for parents to set free the power of blessing over their child's young adult life. I personally like this second version better.

However, I would not call such a celebration a Bar/Bat Mitzvah, because the idea is not to call our children sons and daughters of the commandment. In honor and recognition of the Jewish ceremony, some Christians have begun to conduct a Bar/Bat Berakhah (Hebrew: son/daughter of "my" blessing) celebration to pronounce blessings upon their children.

Whatever you decide to call this special day of celebration, the key idea is to pray over your child. Stand in the authority you have as a parent, and by the guidance of the Holy Spirit, speak blessing over your child. Release and welcome your child into adulthood. Allow opportunity for the newly welcomed adult to pray and testify to all present of their walk with God up to this point.

The Day After

Do not stop being a parent after this day. Your young adult still needs your love, support, supervision, guidance, and protection. However, you might need to change your parenting style to one that allows the full use of responsibility. Your young adult needs to have the freedom to make gradually bigger, and therefore more consequential, decisions. Allow for mistakes to gain wisdom, but naturally, only to the extent that is reasonable, safe, and in line with the Word of God. They are still living under your roof. Stand firm if you're challenged and be clear in saying, "As for me and my house, we serve the Lord."

> So fear the Lord and serve him wholeheartedly. Put away forever the idols your ancestors worshiped when they lived beyond the Euphrates River and in Egypt. Serve the Lord alone. But if you refuse to serve the Lord, then choose today whom you will serve. Would you prefer the gods your ancestors served beyond the Euphrates? Or will it be the gods of the Amorites in whose land you now live? But as for me and my family, we will serve the Lord (Joshua 24:14–15).

Jewish children do not neglect the studies of the scriptures after their Bar/Bat Mitzvah. Neither should your child. You will still guide the child's decisions and spiritual development. With this in mind, your child needs to step out onto the water. Peter dared to walk on the water to get closer to Jesus. He discovered the importance of always having his eyes fixed on Jesus. You can only share the delight of seeing your child walk on the water if you let them. What joy it will be when you will see your child reaching out to cling onto the hand of Christ.

Bar Mitzvah
Traditional Jewish Version (Summarized)
History and Traditions

As we have learned, Bar Mitzvah "son of the commandment" refers to a boy who has reached thirteen years of age. It is then that he is considered responsible enough to take on the religious obligations of Jewish life. While a special religious service or ceremony is not required to become a bar mitzvah, it has over the centuries become increasingly emphasized as a "rite of passage."

The earliest Bar Mitzvah observance held was simply the boy being called on to recite the Torah at the first Torah service after his thirteenth birthday. Today, the Bar Mitzvah ceremony usually entails much more preparation and participation from the boy. He works with the Rabbi for months, even years, studying for the event. The exact role of the boy at his Bar Mitzvah varies greatly between the Jewish movements and synagogues.

Typically today, this event includes the following elements:

Reading In
The Torah

- Reading the portion of the Torah (five books of Moses) in Hebrew that is prescribed for that week and chanting the Haftarah (corresponding portion from the Prophets for that week).
- Reciting the benediction before and after the reading which is called the Aliyah, meaning "to rise, to ascend or to go up."
- Giving an interpretation of the readings.
- Leading parts of or all of the prayer services.
- Completing a fundraiser project to a charity of his choice.

Rabbi Shalomo Luria was a teacher of Jewish law in the sixteenth century. Next to many works, he was known for his *Talmudic* commentary. Rabbi Shalom Luria notes that the occasion of a youth becoming obligated to obey the commandments is to be celebrated with a religious feast. In this customary Bar Mitzvah meal, the parents give thanks and praise to God for giving them the merit to raise a child to Bar Mitzvah and to educate him in the ways of Torah and the commandments.

Bat Mitzvah
Traditional Jewish Version (Summarized)
Bat Mitzvah—Rights And Responsibilities

At twelve years of age, a girl becomes a *bat mitzvah* and is recognized by Jewish tradition as having the same rights as an adult. As such, she has the right to own property or enter into a contract. In traditional Jewish law, a girl can technically be married when she becomes a Bat Mitzvah. Some Jews talk about becoming a Bat

Mitzvah as "becoming a woman" or bar mitzvah as "becoming a man." This is not correct. A Bat Mitzvah has many of the rights and responsibilities of a Jewish adult, but she is not yet considered an adult in the full sense of the word.

In the *Mishnah,* Avot 5:21, a thirteen-year-old is listed as the age of responsibility for the *mitzvoth.* However, the age for marriage is set at eighteen and the age for earning a living at twenty. Therefore, a Bat Mitzvah is not a full-fledged adult yet, but Jewish tradition recognizes this age as the point when a child can differentiate between right and wrong and hence can be held accountable for her actions.

Jewish children are not required to perform *mitzvoth* (plural for mitzvah, meaning a precept or commandment). While they are encouraged to fulfill as many mitzvoth as possible, the commandments are not obligatory until a girl becomes bat mitzvah. In traditional Jewish practice, a girl who has become bat mitzvah must observe mitzvoth just like any adult woman. These includes, but is not limited to, lighting Shabbat candles, fasting on Yom Kippur, and performing acts of charity.

Bat Mitzvah Ceremony

Bat Mitzvah also refers to the religious ceremony in the synagogue that accompanies a girl becoming a Bat Mitzvah. Often a celebratory party will follow the ceremony, which is also called a Bat Mitzvah. The specifics of the ceremony and party vary widely depending on which movement of Judaism the family belongs to.

In the late nineteenth and early twentieth centuries, many Jewish communities began marking when a girl became a Bat Mitzvah with a special ceremony. This was a break from traditional Jewish custom, which prohibited women from participating directly in religious services. Using the Bar Mitzvah (boy) ceremony as a model, Jews in more liberal communities began to experiment with developing a similar ceremony for girls. Today, Bat Mitzvah has even become more common among Orthodox Jews.

Although most Bat Mitzvah ceremonies are on Saturday morning, some congregations also do Bat Mitzvah services on Friday nights by following the traditions of their particular synagogue. The girl becoming a Bat Mitzvah will read from the Torah and lead some prayers at a Torah Service. She will then give her personal interpretation of her Torah portion in a speech. In some communities, the girl may also need to complete a charity project leading up to the ceremony to raise money or donations for a charity of her choice.

Bat Mitzvah Party And Gifts

Usually, following the Bat Mitzvah ceremony, invited guests will attend a celebratory lunch. Some families developed this celebration into a grand party. There may be music playing and dance. However, this is a more recent development and has not caught on among Orthodox communities. Gifts or cash are commonly given to a Bat Mitzvah usually after the ceremony or meal. Portions of any monetary gifts are often given the future education of the Bat Mitzvah.

Time With God

Mom & Dad

God entrusted us as parents with the great call of raising our children. You are stepping into a unique partnership with God. What do I mean? God wants to be a normal everyday part of your family. He is always present and enjoys leading you in your conquest of raising your child.

Every Christian parent seeks God for wisdom. Some of our prayers are very simple. They originate deep within our heart and can be very passionate and short. They go something like this: "Help, God."

This chapter of "Time With God" is intended to do exactly that, to have a time with God in prayer, to seek Him for wisdom. Pour out to God in prayer your concerns, fears, and questions (Philippians 4:7–7).

Discover what God has to say in His word, the Bible, about the following eight points:

1. Knowing Your Child's Strengths

God has given each of our children different gifts and interests that will make them special, unique, individual. Our focus must be on these gifts so that we can build them up to excel and be released in these areas of strength. This will set free enthusiasm, passion, and joy (Psalm 139; Philippians 1:6; 1 Corinthians 12).

Directed by our human nature, we fix our eyes too easily on shortcomings, weaknesses, and sin. In doing so, we are hindering the work of God's grace in our child. The child is tempted to equally focus on his/her weaknesses. We ought to be faithful in our strengths and gifts God has given us. He does not expect us to be perfect in every area. Neither should we expect it from our child (Romans 12:6).

2. Rules/Laws

Here are some basic but nevertheless guiding thoughts about family rules. Rules are, in essence, nothing more than the "family laws." These rules/laws reflect the boundaries and guiding values of our family. Galatians reveals a key verse to help us understand the laws and commandments recorded in the Old Testament. It is written that the law is given to lead us to Jesus Christ. Our rules should reflect the same.

> Therefore, the Law has become our tutor to
> lead us to Christ, so that we may be justified by
> faith. (Galatians 3:24)

Recognize that God's justice and His laws are perfect. Justice and the law cannot be without love and mercy. Love and mercy cannot be without the law and justice. A failing of either side would end in perfect cruelty. God keeps both sides in perfect balance. Typically, if you lean toward law and justice, your kids might observe you as cold and distant and react in this way toward you. If you lean toward love and mercy, they might be tempted to take advantage of that. The child will take charge of the family by serving his own selfish interests. In your family, you stand in the center of both sides to keep them in balance. Reflect on the following Bible passages regarding law, justice, mercy, faithfulness, and the love of God.

> Woe to you, scribes and Pharisees, hypocrites! For you tithe mint and dill and cumin, and have neglected the weightier provisions of the law: justice and mercy and faithfulness; but these are the things you should have done without neglecting the others. (Matthew 23:23)

> What sorrow awaits you Pharisees! For you are careful to tithe even the tiniest income from your herb gardens, but you ignore justice and the love of God. You should tithe, yes, but do not neglect the more important things. (Luke 11:42)

We are challenged in today's world in so many ways. Our prayers often cry out, "Oh, God, give me wisdom so I am able to make a good and wise decision." Saying "no" or creating a new rule may indeed be the right thing. Nevertheless, guard yourself from giving new rules too quickly based on a hasty and emotional first reaction. All too often, our rules and decisions reflect our laziness, tiredness, stubbornness, fears, hurts, or maybe even the unwillingness to deal with a problem. Ask yourself why you are saying no or making the rule. Will it benefit my child and lead them toward Christ? What is my child seeing?

It is a testimony of God's greatness that He instructed the Israelites to live by just ten commandments. They are short, simple, and straightforward. And even these ten are based on only two commandments. Listen to what Jesus has to say:

> "Teacher, which is the most important commandment in the Law of Moses?" Jesus replied, "'You must love the Lord your God with all your heart, all your soul, and all your mind.' This is the first and greatest commandment. A second is equally important: 'Love your neighbor as yourself.' The entire law and all the demands of the prophets are based on these two commandments." (Matthew 22:36–40)

Consider doing the same with your family rules—keep them short, simple, and straightforward. Keep in mind that the rules/laws should keep our children safe and pure. Depending on your situation and the child's age, you may want to include them in the process of making these rules, especially when it comes to formulating the consequences if rules are broken.

Every law and rule will be challenged! It hasn't changed since Adam and Eve broke God's rule in the garden. "Do not" seems to stir up in us the question of "what if." This "what if" is accompanied by doubts of God's perfect love and plan for us. The law or our rules may actually arouse in our children their sinful passions (such as rebellion) according to Romans.

> For while we were in the flesh, the sinful passions, which were aroused by the Law, were at work in the members of our body to bear fruit for death. (Romans 7:5)

You may ask, if that is so, do our children need to have rules and boundaries? In short, *yes!* Rules and boundaries define and communicate identity, value, and security. Without them, a child runs wild and astray from God's will and plan. You as the parent are held responsible to uphold discipline in your family. Eli refused to rebuke, restrain, or discipline his sons, even after God warned him about it. We learn from the Bible that Eli's failure impacted the entire nation. Do not underestimate the value of right and wrong, the value of rules/laws in your family. Know and uphold the will of God for and in your family. You never know how your family values might impact a nation in the future!

> Then the Lord said to Samuel, "I am about to do a shocking thing in Israel. I am going to carry out all my threats against Eli and his family, from beginning to end. I have warned him (*Eli*) that judgment is coming upon his family forever, because his sons are blaspheming God and he hasn't disciplined them (*rebuke them, NASB/did not restrain them, NKJV*). So I have vowed that the sins of Eli and his sons will never be forgiven by sacrifices or offerings." (1 Samuel 3:11–14)

> "Israel has been defeated by the Philistines," the messenger replied. "The people have been slaughtered, and your two sons, Hophni and Phinehas, were also killed. And the Ark of God has been captured." (1 Samuel 4:17)

> When the messenger mentioned what had happened to the Ark of God, Eli fell backward from his seat beside the gate. He broke his neck and died, for he was old and overweight. He had been Israel's judge for forty years. Eli's daughter–in–law, the wife of Phinehas, was pregnant and near her time of delivery. When she heard that the Ark of God had been captured and that her father–in–law and husband were dead, she went into labor and gave birth. She died in childbirth, but before she passed away the midwives tried to encourage her. "Don't be afraid," they said. "You have a baby boy!" But she did not answer or pay attention to them. She named the child Ichabod (which means "Where is the glory?"),

for she said, "Israel's glory is gone." She named
him this because the Ark of God had been
captured and because her father–in–law and
husband were dead. Then she said, "The glory
has departed from Israel, for the Ark of God has
been captured." (1 Samuel 4:19–22)

Rules should lead the children to Christ. God's law will make
itself known to the conscience of our believing children should they
fall into sin. It is like a safety alert so that they would not fall farther
into deeper decay. Our children have a great calling by God's grace
to live by a higher standard than could ever be achieved by the law.
The law works from the outside, the Holy Spirit from the inside. The
Holy Spirit is able to bring change to our children by His grace and
power.

Therefore, there is now no condemnation
for those who are in Christ Jesus. For the law of
the Spirit of life in Christ Jesus has set you free
from the law of sin and of death. (Romans 8:1–2)

The closer children grow in their relationship with the Lord
Jesus Christ, the more they will automatically live by a much higher
standard than our family rules. Our family rules are at this time not
eliminated; rather they serve as guardian if any one of the family
should fall.

So then, the law was our guardian until
Christ came, in order that we might be justified
by faith. But now that faith has come, we are no
longer under a guardian, for in Christ Jesus you
are all sons of God, through faith. (Galatians
3:24–26)

Our aim as parents is not to control our children with rules, but
to guide them into an abiding relationship with God. It is therefore

necessary that each child learns what it means to abide in Christ, to depend and trust in His grace, and to learn to hear Gods voice. As our children become better acquainted with the Word of God, the Holy Spirit will sharpen their ability to recognize God in their own hearts. Peace and strength are found in daily communion with God. The rich flow of God's grace will indeed amplify their moral excellence, self-control, kindness, and love. They will develop a longing to see with spiritual eyes what Jesus is doing in their own lives and in the world.

Text: Galatians 3:10–29; Galatians 4, 5

3. Stumbled or Failed

Children are not a separate unidentifiable entity in the body of Christ. They are our children and yet also our brothers and sisters in Christ. Ephesians 4 speaks about bringing sorrow to God's Holy Spirit by the way we live. We should get rid of all bitterness, rage, anger, harsh words, and slander as well as all types of evil behavior. Instead, we ought to be kind to each other, tenderhearted, forgiving one another—just as God through Christ has forgiven us. Are we living this out in the relationships we have with our children? If we have stumbled or failed, we can know that there is freedom found in Christ. Curses can be broken, forgiveness given and received, and healing experienced in Jesus Christ.

4. Guilt and Pride

A parent's greatest moment is to see every one of their children following Jesus Christ passionately and without compromise. Nevertheless, not everyone in the family may be at the same stage in their personal relationship with Jesus Christ. This might stretch from one child that expresses a very exciting faith in Christ to their sibling whose heartbeat of faith is hardly recognizable. And yes, one child might not believe in Christ at all. You may find yourself having times of guilt or condemnation, blaming yourself for your shortcomings that not all of your children are strong Christians.

Another family might have a completely different situation. In this family, everyone is saved and follows Christ. What are the hidden traps here? Be aware of pride. Why? Think about it. Was it your marvelous parenting method that saved your child? No! It was the working of the Holy Spirit. This truth does not make light of the fact of how God used you. Your impact may have been very significant. You were faithful with what God showed you in your family. Nonetheless, if you are thinking more about yourself than simply a servant and channel of God's grace, you need to get rid of your pride and thank God for the grace He bestowed on your family.

But what about your guilt? Sorry, it is not about you. It is about the work of the Holy Spirit. What God is looking for in you is an open, tender, and humble heart that is willing to listen and obey as you abide in Jesus Christ. In Christ, you will be able to walk in the perfect plan that God has laid out for your family. It will be by His grace, timing, and power. Ask God if you need to repent so that He can have His way in your family.

> God the Father knew you and chose you long ago, and his spirit has made you holy. As a result, you have obeyed him and have been cleansed by the blood of Jesus Christ. (1 Peter 1:2)

> God the Father planned long ago to choose you (chose you according to his foreknowledge) by making you his holy people, which is the Spirit's work (or by the sanctifying / purifying work of the Spirit; or by setting you apart by means of the Spirit). God wanted you to obey him and to be made clean (sprinkled) by the blood of the death of Jesus Christ. (In the Old Testament blood from animal sacrifices was sprinkled on persons and objects to indicate purification or forgiveness

of sins; Exodus 24:3–8.) (1 Peter 1:2, Expanded Bible).

King David had his share of problems with his family. Not everything was perfect. This did not limit God from releasing His blessing upon David's repenting heart after committing adultery and murder. God chose Uriah's wife, whose husband David killed, to be the lineage from which Christ was born.

> And Jesse the father of David the king. And David was the father of Solomon by the wife of Uriah. (Matthew 1:6)

Moreover, God spoke of David:

> After removing Saul, he made David their king. God testified concerning him: "I have found David, son of Jesse, a man after my own heart; he will do everything I want him to do." (Acts 13:22)

5. I Love You

Three fundamental words that make a world of difference. Use them generously and honestly mean it. Be attentive when and how you say it. Too easily we say them only in connection with some praiseworthy achievement. If so, the child will most likely connect your love with good performance. Therefore use these words: "I love you;" likewise, when the child is doing nothing in particular (such as playing alone, etc.). God's love is unconditional. Let us follow His example.

We know from the Bible that God also communicated His love to His son. Listen:

> And a voice from heaven said, "This is my dearly loved Son, who brings me great joy." (Matthew 3:17)

> But even as he spoke, a bright cloud overshadowed them, and a voice from the cloud said, "This is my dearly loved Son, who brings me great joy. Listen to him." (Matthew 17:5)

Your actions are important and will communicate your love. Your family requires your undivided personal time. In many cases, that demands vigorous planning from Mom and Dad. Quality time with your child is not achieved by planning alone. I believe it is rather about your commitment to choose the right opportunities—when your child asks you to play, to talk about something, to read a story, to cook something together, or to come to a school event. Those are the right times.

I was always amazed how easily interaction turned into great fun and quality time with our children by simply listening. This is what denying yourself means. And this will give you practice. Say no to your favorite TV show. Say no to playing on your electronic devices such as phone, tablets, PlayStation or computer. Say no to a well-deserved rest on the sofa. Say no to your favorite excuse. It is time to play with your child!

Ask your child what you do that makes them feel loved. What is it that communicates your love? You will be surprised to hear what they perceive as love. By the way, you can also share what nonverbal things communicate love to you. It might well be one of those big bear hugs from your child. I absolutely loved to roughhouse with my kids. We rolled down the hills in the grass. We piled up onto each other and made a family "sandwich." We laughed and screamed with excitement. We learned later from our kids that this roughhousing was by far number one for them. It towered over everything else that communicated "nonverbal love." I was absolutely surprised.

For all you moms, yes, we had some simple rules about rough-housing and playing like that—no broken bones, no gushing blood, not in the kitchen, and stop means stop! And yes, I was the one that got in trouble the most, and not the kids. I was rightfully accused of initiating such fun times right before bedtime. Naturally, this concern did not initiate from the kids. They (and I) could have gone on all night.

6. An Arrow in God's Hand

The Bible itself does not define the age by which children become responsible in God's eyes. Based on the tradition of Bar / Bat Mitzvah, we can expect our children to hear directly from the Lord for themselves and be directly responsible to Him in their early teens. While God can speak to us at any age, they are now responsible to react upon His word. Therefore, we need to have diligently trained our children prior to their twelfth or thirteenth year. Then they need to know how to recognize the voice of the Holy Spirit within their own hearts, make wise decisions, and develop an attitude of submission. With this in place, our children will be prepared to take their place as young adults, as sons and daughters of blessing in the kingdom of God.

We learned that Bar/Bat Mitzvah does not mean being a full adult in every sense of the word. We need to continue to be a channel of God's grace in the lives of our young adults. How precious it is to see God's work manifested in our children. Let us be thankful and remember how God poured into our children His Word, character, and heart, to see where they have found confidence in their ability to hear from Him by which they are now able to make wise decisions.

The time will come to release them into God's hand so that he would continue the work of grace and calling on our children. God has given us children for a purpose. An arrow is not intended to remain in the quiver. An arrow is meant to be released. The arrow (child) does not achieve its destiny until the warrior (God) takes aim and lets it go, released into their future of His calling for your child. Are we willing to let God aim the arrow—our child—into the direction of His choosing?

> Children are a gift from the Lord; they are a reward from him. Children born to a young man are like arrows in a warrior's hands. How joyful is the man whose quiver is full of them! He will not be put to shame when he confronts his accusers at the city gates. (Psalm 127:3–5)

Isaiah speaks of God's calling as well:

> Listen to me, all you in distant lands! Pay attention, you who are far away! The Lord called me before my birth; from within the womb he called me by name. He made my words of judgment as sharp as a sword. He has hidden me in the shadow of his hand. I am like a sharp arrow in his quiver. He said to me, "You are my servant, Israel, and you will bring me glory." (Isaiah 49:1–3)

7. Forgiveness

In order to maintain healthy relationships, we need to know how to respond to people that hurt us. Each family members' actions and words carry, in particular, the power to inflict deep and painful wounds. The answer is revealed by Christ and stands unshakable, fair and simple. We have to forgive. To forgive may appear, in our eyes, impossible or even unjust.

A wise man once explained it this way: not to forgive is like eating rat poison with the hope the other person will die. May God help us see the power, blessing, and privilege of forgiveness.

Peter also struggled with forgiveness. Nevertheless, he made an outstanding and wise decision. Peter went to Jesus with his problem.

> Then Peter came to him (Jesus) and asked, "Lord, how often should I forgive someone who sins against me? Seven times?" "No, not seven

times," Jesus replied, "but seventy times seven!" (Matthew 18:21–22)

Within Judaism, three times was sufficient to show a forgiving spirit (based on Job 33:29,30; Amos 1:3, 2:6). Thus Peter (seven times) believed he had shown generosity. But true disciples of Jesus are to forgive without keeping count (seventy times seven). The Bible doesn't reveal Peter's reaction, maybe because Peter looked so puzzled. Jesus continued with the parable of the unforgiving debtor.

Therefore, the Kingdom of heaven can be compared to a king who decided to bring his accounts up to date with servants who had borrowed money from him. In the process, one of his debtors was brought in who owed him millions of dollars. He couldn't pay, so his master ordered that he be sold—along with his wife, his children, and everything he owned—to pay the debt. But the man fell down before his master and begged him, "Please, be patient with me, and I will pay it all."

Then his master was filled with pity for him, and he released him and forgave his debt. But when the man left the king, he went to a fellow servant who owed him a few thousand dollars. He grabbed him by the throat and demanded instant payment. His fellow servant fell down before him and begged for a little more time. "Be patient with me, and I will pay it," he pleaded.

But his creditor wouldn't wait. He had the man arrested and put in prison until the debt could be paid in full. When some of the other servants saw this, they were very upset. They went to the king and told him everything that had happened. Then the king called in the man he had forgiven and said, "You evil servant! I forgave you that tremendous debt because you pleaded with me. Shouldn't you have mercy on your fellow servant, just as I had mercy on you?" Then the angry king sent the man to prison to be tortured until he had paid his entire debt. That's what my heavenly Father will do to you if you refuse to forgive your brothers and sisters from your heart. (Matthew 18:23–34)

Do we realize how hopelessly lost we were in our sins? Do we understand how much God forgave us? Forgiveness is possible because the price for our sins was paid on the cross. We must be willing to make a conscious decision to extend forgiveness to others. Forgiving will release the grip the past has on us, clear the record of what we hold against others, and break any resentment. This is the only way to freedom.

The poison of unforgiveness will impact and spread far beyond your relationship with the offender. Therefore, be wise and let God show you how you've reacted to offenses, also including your own relationship with God. Unforgiveness in us tends to give birth to an array of other sins. Perhaps you are upset/offended at something you thought God should've done differently. When is the last time you used words like *never again, always, that's the last time*, etc.? Or has unforgiveness led you to be entangled in sinful ties with others? And, not at the least, with what have you comforted your pain? The human heart is very creative in comforting or covering pain.

After you have renounced and broken any vows, asked God for forgiveness for sins, severed any sinful ties, and have specifically forgiven the offense, you enter into a crucial but absolutely wonderful time. Your wounds need healing from the Gentle Healer, as songwriter Micheal Card affectionally expressed. God is waiting for you to take you in His arms, to heal and comfort you. Trust yourself to His care. Listen to Him. He will guide you.

Why is this so crucial? When feeling the old pain, you might tend to constantly question yourself if you really have completely forgiven. You might be tempted to run in circles by forgiving again and again the same thing. Furthermore, human nature will automatically try to ease and comfort pain with sin. Get to know your Gentle Healer. He is able to heal and set you free. You will enjoy your freedom. Celebrate!

You can pray through the process of repentance, forgiveness, and healing alone with God (or if you like, with a close Christian friend). The person that offended you is not physically present. The exception is if the person personally approaches you and asks you for your forgiveness. Do not prolong your answer, but quickly grant your wholehearted forgiveness. Forgiveness is not carried out by a feeling but by a decision.

Also ask God to help you understand your reactions to those that offend you. Sometimes our reactions are not pleasing in God's eyes. We might need to bring things in order with the offender. The goal of this is not to explain the offense to the offender but to ask forgiveness for how you treated the offender. God will show you if this step is needed and what you should say.

Are we aware of our own sins? Do we take action and apologize? Too many people are frightened to expose weakness. The list of reasons why not to apologize gets longer and longer with time. Understand that any sin will expose itself eventually. It is only a matter of time.

In today's society, common courtesies are ever so often dimmed by self-centered ignorance and fears. We need to learn that our action, or the lack thereof, impacts other people. Saying you're sorry is taking responsibility for mistakes. People around you will recognize it and place greater trust in you. That includes your children. Learning and making mistakes go hand in hand. It takes time to learn something new. It is not expected from you to apologize every time you have a mishap. Unfortunately, if a person—and it might be you—is corrected for endlessly apologizing, they stop saying sorry altogether. Don't let your heart be hardened because you were corrected. Learn and be sensitive to the leading of the Holy Spirit. He knows when you need to say something.

Every person reacts differently to pain. On one side of the spectrum, you find a person that faithfully lives out forgiveness and praise. It is simply a normal everyday spiritual exercise. And then there is the other side. For this person, forgiveness is an unthinkable great challenge. Of course, there are many variations in between the two. Where do you stand? The Bible verses below speak about forgiveness, healing, praise, and holy living. Ponder upon these and let God speak to your heart.

> Work at living in peace with everyone, and work at living a holy life, for those who are not holy will not see the Lord. Look after each other so that none of you fails to receive the grace of God. Watch out that no poisonous root of bitterness grows up to trouble you, corrupting many. (Hebrews 12:14–15)

> Vengeance is Mine, and retribution, In due time their foot will slip; For the day of their calamity is near, And the impending things are hastening upon them. (Deuteronomy 32:35)

> Beloved, never avenge yourselves, but leave it to the wrath of God, for it is written, "Vengeance is mine, I will repay, says the Lord." (Romans 12:19)

> People ruin their lives by their own foolishness and then are angry at the Lord. (Proverbs 19:3)

> A cheerful heart is good medicine, but a broken spirit saps a person's strength. (Proverbs 17:22)

> A glad heart makes a happy face; a broken heart crushes the spirit. (Proverbs 15:13)

An evil man is held captive by his own sins; they are ropes that catch and hold him. He will die for lack of self-control; he will be lost because of his great foolishness. (Proverbs 5:22–23)

Kind words are like honey—sweet to the soul and healthy for the body. (Proverbs 16:24)

Oh, what joy for those whose disobedience is forgiven, whose sin is put out of sight! Yes, what joy for those whose record the Lord has cleared of guilt, whose lives are lived in complete honesty! When I refused to confess my sin, my body wasted away, and I groaned all day long. Day and night your hand of discipline was heavy on me. My strength evaporated like water in the summer heat. Finally, I confessed all my sins to you and stopped trying to hide my guilt. I said to myself, "I will confess my rebellion to the Lord." And you forgave me! All my guilt is gone. (Psalm 32)

Let all that I am praise the Lord; with my whole heart, I will praise his holy name. Let all that I am praise the Lord; may I never forget the good things he does for me. He forgives all my sins and heals all my diseases. He redeems me from death and crowns me with love and tender mercies. He fills my life with good things. My youth is renewed like the eagle's! The Lord gives righteousness and justice to all who are treated unfairly. (Psalm 103:1–6)

How wonderful and pleasant it is when brothers live together in harmony! For harmony is as precious as the anointing oil that was poured over Aaron's head, that ran down his beard and onto the border of his robe. Harmony is as refreshing as the dew from Mount Hermon that falls on the mountains of Zion. And there the Lord has pronounced his blessing, even life everlasting. (Psalm 133)

Don't worry about the wicked or envy those who do wrong. For like grass, they soon fade away. Like spring flowers, they soon wither. Trust in the Lord and do good. Then you will live safely in the land and prosper. Take delight in the Lord, and he will give you your heart's desires. Commit everything you do to the Lord. Trust him, and he will help you. He will make your innocence radiate like the dawn, and the justice of your cause will shine like the noonday sun. Be still in the presence of the Lord, and wait patiently for him to act. Don't worry about evil people who prosper or fret about their wicked schemes. Stop being angry! Turn from your rage! Do not lose your temper—it only leads to harm. For the wicked will be destroyed, but those who trust in the Lord will possess the land. Soon the wicked will disappear. Though you look for them, they will be gone. The lowly will possess the land and will live in peace and prosperity. The wicked plot against the godly; they snarl at them in defiance. But the Lord just laughs, for he sees their day of judgment coming. The wicked draw their swords and string their bows to kill the poor and the oppressed, to slaughter those who do right. But their swords will stab their own hearts, and their bows will be broken. It is better to be godly and have little than to be evil and rich. For the strength of the wicked will be shattered, but the Lord takes care of the godly.

Day by day the Lord takes care of the innocent, and they will receive an inheritance that lasts forever. They will not be disgraced in hard times; even in famine they will have more than enough. But the wicked will die. The Lord's enemies are like flowers in a field—they will disappear like smoke. The wicked borrow and never repay, but the godly are generous givers. Those the Lord blesses will possess the land, but those he curses will die. The Lord directs the steps of the godly. He delights in every detail of their lives. Though they stumble, they will never fall, for the Lord holds them by the hand. Once I was young, and now I am old. Yet I have never seen the godly abandoned or their children begging for bread. The godly always give generous loans to others, and their children are a blessing. Turn from evil and do good, and you will live in the land forever. For the Lord loves justice, and he will never abandon the godly. He will keep them safe forever, but the children of the wicked will die. The godly will possess the land and will live there forever. The godly offer good counsel; they teach right from wrong. They have made God's law their own, so they will never slip from his path. The wicked wait in ambush for the godly, looking for an excuse to kill them. But the Lord will not let the wicked succeed or let the godly be condemned when they are put on trial. Put your hope in the Lord. Travel steadily along his path. He will honor you by giving you the land. You will see the wicked destroyed. I have seen wicked and ruthless people flourishing like a tree in its native soil. But when I looked again, they were gone! Though I searched for them, I could not find them! Look at those who are honest and good, for a wonderful future awaits those who love peace. But the rebellious will be destroyed; they have no future. The Lord rescues the godly; he is their fortress in times of trouble. The Lord helps them, rescuing them from the wicked. He saves them, and they find shelter in him. (Psalm 37)

Praise the Lord! How good to sing praises to our God! How delightful and how fitting! The Lord is rebuilding Jerusalem and bringing the exiles back to Israel. He heals the brokenhearted and bandages their wounds. He counts the stars and calls them all by name. How great is our Lord! His power is absolute! His understanding is beyond comprehension! The Lord supports the humble, but he brings the wicked down into the dust. (Psalm 147:1–6)

O Lord, if you heal me, I will be truly healed; if you save me, I will be truly saved. My praises are for you alone! (Jeremiah 17:14)

You may think you can condemn such people, but you are just as bad, and you have no excuse! When you say they are wicked and should be punished, you are condemning yourself, for you who judge others do these very same things. And we know that God, in his justice, will punish anyone who does such things. Since you judge others for doing these things, why do you think you can avoid God's judgment when you do the same things? Don't you see how wonderfully kind, tolerant, and patient God is with you? Does this mean nothing to you? Can't you see that his kindness is intended to turn you from your sin? (Romans 2:1–4)

> Don't copy the behavior and customs of this world, but let God transform you into a new person by changing the way you think. Then you will learn to know God's will for you, which is good and pleasing and perfect. (Romans 12:2)

Having adversaries comes with the territory of being a Christian. It would not be wise to think that the enemy has no interest in us. Sometimes we know perfectly well who it is that is working against us, and sometimes we only reap the effects of his schemes. We could get angry and very easily resentful, especially where we see our hopes and dreams destroyed. Hopelessness and defeat may even poison our thinking. Stop!

We need to forgive the person and recognizing that our fight is a spiritual battle and is fought with spiritual weapons. We need to resist the temptation to see our life through the eyes of our enemy. We keep our hearts pure and see our lives through the eyes of Christ. In doing so, the enemy will fight not against us, but against God.

There is rest found in knowing that we are in the hand of God our heavenly Father and in His loving kindness. The enemy is not able to hold back God's blessing or plans for us no matter how hard he works. Our lives may take a sharp turn. God delights in using the enemy's schemes for our best so that we grow in Him; so that we get to know our heavenly Father and learn to trust in His love, justice, and power. He is God Almighty.

> So my advice is, leave these men alone. Let them go. If they are planning and doing these things merely on their own, it will soon be overthrown. But if it is from God, you will not be able to overthrow them. You may even find yourselves fighting against God! (Acts 5:38–39)

For you will break the yoke of their slavery
and lift the heavy burden from their shoulders.
You will break the oppressor's rod, just as you
did when you destroyed the army of Midian.
For a child is born to us, a son is given to us.
The government will rest on his shoulders. And
he will be called: Wonderful Counselor, Mighty
God, Everlasting Father, Prince of Peace. His
government and its peace will never end. He will
rule with fairness and justice from the throne of
his ancestor David for all eternity. The passionate
commitment of the Lord of heaven's Armies will
make this happen! (Isaiah 9:4,6–7)

Text: Psalm 37:7,34; Psalm 2:1–6; Philippians 4:8

8. Blessing

Giving our blessing, in particular the father's blessing, has
become less practiced in today's Christian world. It is somewhat
peculiar since we all have a longing in our heart to be blessed by our
parents. A hurting or broken relationship with our father will most
likely emphasize what we miss. He in particular has a special role in
our discovery of who we are in life. Affirming, encouraging, praising,
and affectionate life-giving words from the father will weigh heavily in leading the child into a healthy adulthood. This truth works
likewise into the negative. Neglecting or using destructive and hurting words will have a devastating impact in the child's development.
God's desire for us is to have a healed and healthy relationship with
our parents. Are we ready to receive the blessing from our parents?
Are we ready to give our blessing to our children?

We know from the story of Jacob and Esau in the Old Testament
how eager they were to receive the fathers' blessing. These words
of blessing were not just wishful thoughts of a father. These words
were given by God through Isaac. Why? In Genesis 25, we read that

Rebecca inquired of the Lord regarding the children within her. God answered her by explaining that two nations are in her womb and that the older shall serve the younger. Isaac did confirm by his blessing to Jacob what God had many years earlier spoken to Rebecca.

Let us inquire of the Lord regarding our children. Let us be a channel of God's grace to our children by speaking forth blessings in the power and leading of the Holy Spirit and by knowing like Isaac knew that his blessing cannot be revoked but will come to pass.

> Then Isaac trembled violently, and said, "Who was he then that hunted game and brought it to me, so that I ate of all of it before you came, and blessed him? Yes, and he shall be blessed." (Genesis 27:33, NASB)

> And yes, that blessing must stand! (Genesis 27:33, NLT)

CHAPTER 10

THE END

Worthy Is the Lamb

I trust that you have found a deeply rooted joy and love for God. The future may hold moments where you feel alone. Remember that Jesus Christ is always with you. He is the way to the Father and is preparing a place for you.

> Teach these new disciples to obey all the commands I have given you. And be sure of this: I am with you always, even to the end of the age. (Matthew 28:20)

> Don't let your hearts be troubled. Trust in God, and trust also in me. There is more than enough room in my Father's home. If this were not so, would I have told you that I am going to prepare a place for you? When everything is ready, I will come and get you, so that you will always be with me where I am. And you know the way to where I am going. (John 14:1–4)

While we live in a world that often despises or distorts truth we should not be surprised. What is truth? Christ says:

> I am the way, the truth, and the life. No one can come to the Father except through me. (John 14:6)

Jesus Christ is the truth. Rejecting Him is rejecting truth. Stand upon the solid rock that will carry you beyond this world. Don't be dazzled by the world's tempting splendor or grueling woes. I would like to give you the following verses on your way along with some thoughts from Matthew Henry. These verses in Revelation are like a lighthouse which shines by its light, hope, and truth into a stormy world. Let Luke's testimony remind your heart to smile. Enjoy every moment of today. This day is a precious gift from God. May His grace and love that exceeds all of our understanding rest upon you!

> And when he took the scroll, the four living beings and the twenty-four elders fell down before the Lamb. Each one had a harp, and they held gold bowls filled with incense, which are the prayers of God's people. And they sang a new song with these words: "You are worthy to take the scroll and break its seals and open it. For you were slaughtered, and your blood has ransomed people for God from every tribe and language and people and nation. And you have caused them to become a Kingdom of priests for our God. And they will reign on the earth." Then I looked again, and I heard the voices of thousands and millions of angels around the throne and of the living beings and the elders. And they sang in a mighty chorus: "Worthy is the Lamb who was slaughtered—to receive power and riches and wisdom and strength and honor and glory and blessing." And then I heard every creature in heaven and on earth and under the earth and in the sea. They sang: "Blessing and honor and glory and power belong to the one sitting on the throne and to the Lamb forever and ever." And the four living beings said, "Amen!" And the twenty-four elders fell down and worshiped the Lamb. (Revelation 5:8–14)

Consider what Matthew Henry observed:

> It is matter of joy to all the world, to see that God deals with men in grace and mercy through the redeemer. He governs the world, not merely as a Creator, but as our Savior. The harps were instruments of praise; the vials were full of odors, or incense, which signify the prayers of the saints: prayer and praise should always go together. Christ has redeemed his people from the bondage of sin, guilt, and Satan. He has not only purchased liberty for them, but the highest honor and preferment; he made them kings and priests; kings, to rule over their own spirits (old English: thoughts, desirers & actions), and to overcome the world, and the evil one; and he makes them priests; giving them access to himself, and liberty to offer up spiritual sacrifices. What words can more fully declare that Christ is, and ought to be worshipped, equally with the Father, by all creatures, to all eternity! Happy those who shall adore and praise in heaven, and who shall forever bless the Lamb, who delivered and set them apart for himself by his blood. How worthy art thou, O God, Father, Son, and Holy Spirit, of our highest praises! All creatures should proclaim thy greatness, and adore thy majesty.

Songs

I'm Free
Bill & Gloria Gaither

So long I had searched for life's meaning,
Enslaved by the world and my greed;
Then the door of the prison was opened by love,
For the ransom was paid – I was free.
I'm free from the fear of tomorrow,
I'm free from the guilt of the past;
For I've traded my shackles for a glorious song,
I'm Free! Praise the Lord! Free at last!
I'm free from the guilt that I carried,
From that dull empty life I'm set free;
For when I met Jesus, He made me complete,
He forgot how foolish I used to be.
I'm free from the fear of tomorrow,
I'm free from the guilt of the past;
For I've traded my shackles for a glorious song,
I'm Free! Praise the Lord! Free at last!
I'm free from the fear of tomorrow,
I'm free from the guilt of the past;
For I've traded my shackles for a glorious song,
I'm Free! Praise the Lord! Free at last!
I'm Free! Praise the Lord! Free at last!

The Sweetest Words He Ever Said
Joel Hemphill

Like the woman brought to Jesus,
who was taken in her sin,
I was so ashamed of what I'd done
and where I'd been.

Well, justice called for payments
that were more than I could give,
When mercy smiled upon me, saying,
"I forgive."

Chorus
Oh, the sweetest words
He ever said were "I forgive"
Death's sentence then was wiped away,
and I could live,
Well, I like the part where He told about
the mansions He would give,
But the sweetest words
He ever said, were "I forgive."
Now, if you're tired of living
with the wrongs that you have done,
Come on home to Jesus,
you know He's the cleansing one.
In His arms He'll hold you,
and you've just begun to live,
When you hear Him gently whisper,
"I forgive."

The Holy City
Music by Stephen Adams
Words by Frederick E. Weatherly

Last night I lay a sleeping
There came a dream so fair,
I stood in old Jerusalem
Beside the temple there.
I heard the children singing,
And ever as they sang
Me thought the voice of angels
From heaven in answer rang,

Me thought the voice of angels
From heaven in answer rang.
Jerusalem! Jerusalem!
Lift up your gates and sing,
Hosanna in the highest!
Hosanna to your King!
And then me thought my dream was changed,
The streets no longer rang.
Hushed were the glad Hosannas
The little children sang.
The sun grew dark with mystery,
The morn was cold and chill,
As the shadow of a cross arose
Upon a lonely hill,
As the shadow of a cross arose
Upon a lonely hill.
Jerusalem! Jerusalem!
Hark! How the angels sing,
Hosanna in the highest!
Hosanna to your King!
And once again the scene was changed,
New earth there seemed to be.
I saw the Holy City
Beside the tideless sea.
The light of God was on its streets,
The gates were open wide,
And all who would might enter,
And no one was denied.
No need of moon or stars by night,
Or sun to shine by day;
It was the new Jerusalem
That would not pass away,
It was the new Jerusalem
That would not pass away.
Jerusalem! Jerusalem!
Sing for the night is o'er!

Hosanna in the highest!
Hosanna forevermore!

How Great Thou Art
Lyrics: Carl Boberg
English Translation: Stuart K. Hine

O Lord my God,
When I in awesome wonder
Consider all
The world Thy Hand hath made,
I see the stars,
I hear the rolling thunder,
Thy pow'r throughout
The universe displayed;
Refrain:
Then sings my soul,
My Savior God, to Thee,
How great Thou art!
How great Thou art!
Then sings my soul,
My Savior God, to Thee,
How great Thou art!
How great Thou art!
When through the woods
And forest glades I wander
I hear the birds
Sing sweetly in the trees;
When I look down
From lofty mountain grandeur
And hear the brook
And feel the gentle breeze;
And when I think,
That God, His Son not sparing;
Sent Him to die,

I scarce can take it in;
That on the Cross,
My burden gladly bearing,
He bled and died
To take away my sin.
When Christ shall come,
With shouts of acclamation,
And take me home,
What joy shall fill my heart!
Then I shall bow
In humble adoration
And there proclaim,
"My God, how great Thou art!"

My Jesus, I Love Thee

Lyricist: W. R. Featherston
Composer: A. J. Gordon

My Jesus, I love Thee, I know Thou art mine;
For Thee all the follies of sin I resign.
My gracious Redeemer, my Savior art Thou;
If ever I loved Thee, my Jesus, 'tis now.
I love Thee because Thou has first loved me,
And purchased my pardon on Calvary's tree.
I love Thee for wearing the thorns on Thy brow;
If ever I loved Thee, my Jesus, 'tis now.
I'll love Thee in life, I will love Thee in death,
And praise Thee as long as Thou lendest me breath;
An empty grave is there to prove my Savior lives.
And say when the death dew lies cold on my brow,
If ever I loved Thee, my Jesus, 'tis now.
In mansions of glory and endless delight,
I'll ever adore Thee in heaven so bright;
I'll sing with the glittering crown on my brow;
If ever I loved Thee, my Jesus, 'tis now.

Somebody Loves Me
W. F. Crumley

I'm in love with my Savior and He's in love with me,
He is with me from day to day, what a friend is He,
Watches over me while I sleep, hears me when I
pray,
I'm as happy as I can be, and I now can say:
Refrain:
Somebody loves me, answers my prayers,
I love Somebody, I know He cares;
Somebody tells me not to repine,
That Somebody is Jesus, and I know He's mine.
You'll be happy if you will let Jesus have His way,
He has work for us all to do every passing day;
Feed the hungry and cheer the sad, for the sinner
pray;
You'll have joy that you never had, and you then
can say:
Then at last when our work is done, He will call
us home
To a mansion He has prepared, nevermore to roam;
We'll sit down by the riverside, cares all passed away,
And with never a pain to bear, what a happy day.

Because He Lives
Composer: William
J. Gaither, Gloria Gaither

God sent His Son, they called Him Jesus
He came to love, heal, and forgive
He lived and died to buy my pardon
An empty grave is there to prove my Savior lives.
Because He lives I can face tomorrow
Because He lives all fear is gone

Because I know He holds the future
And life is worth the living just because He lives.
How sweet to hold a newborn baby
And feel the pride, a joy he gives
But greater still the calm assurance
This child can face uncertain days because He
lives.
Because He lives I can face tomorrow
Because He lives all fear is gone
Because I know He holds the future
And life is worth the living just because He lives.
And then one day I'll cross the river
I'll fight life's final war with pain
And then as death gives way to vict'ry
I'll see the lights of glory and I'll know He lives.
Because He lives I can face tomorrow
Because He lives all fear is gone
Because I know He holds the future
And life is worth the living just because He lives.

RESOURCE INDEX

Resources for Chapter 2
Helyer, Larry R. 2002. *Exploring Jewish Literature of the Second Temple Period*. Illinois: Inter Varsity Press

Resources for Chapter 3,5,8,9
Conner, Kevin J. 1980. *The Feasts of Israel*. Portland, Oregon: City Bible Publishing.

Resources for Chapter: 3,5,8,9
Buksbazen, Victor. 1954, 1992, 1999. *The Feast of Israel*. Fort Washington, Pennsylvania: Christian Literature Crusade
Zimmerman, Martha. 2004. *Celebrating Biblical Feasts*. South Bloomington, Minnesota: Bethany House Publishers.
Booker, Richard. 1987. Jesus in the Feasts of Israel. Shippensburg, Pennsylvania: Sounds of the Trumpet, Inc.
Parsons, John J. 2003–2018. "Hebrews for Christians: Study Notes." http://www.hebrew4christians.com

Resources for Chapter: 6
Murray, Andrew. 1979. *Abide in Christ*. New Kensington, Pennsylvania: Whitaker House.

Resources for Chapter: 4,9
Virkler, Mark & Patti. 2005. *How to Hear God's Voice*. Shippensburg, Pennsylvania: Destiny Image Publishers, Inc.

Resources for Chapter: 5,9
Virkler, Mark & Patti. 1990, 2003. *Naturally Supernatural*. Lama Publishing.

Resources for Chapter: 7
Bullinger, E. W. 1984. *Commentary on Revelation*. Grand Rapids, Michigan: Kernel Publications

Resources for Chapter: 9
Virkler, Mark & Patti. 2002. *Rivers of Grace*. England: Sovereign World Ltd.

Resources for Chapter: 4,6
Krupp, Nate. 1998. *Getting to Know God*. Salem, Oregon: Preparing the Way Publishers.

Resources for Chapter: 3
Nelson, Thomas. 2010–2011. *God's Promises for Graduates*. Nashville, Tennessee: Thomas Nelson, Inc.

Resources for Chapter: 4,6,7
Mac Arthur, John. 2005. The Mac Arthur Bible Commentary, Nashville, Tennessee: Thomas Nelson, Inc.

Resources for Chapter: 2,4,6,7
Study Notes:
The ESV Study Bible, English Standard Version (ESV) © Copyright 2008 by Crossway Bibles, A publishing ministry of good news publishers the holy bible, English Standard Version (ESV) © Copyright 2001 by Crossway Bibles, Publishing Ministry of Good News Publishers ESV, Tex edition 2007

ABOUT THE AUTHOR

Bible scholar Dr. Werner Sonderegger served on the mission field in Europe and Africa. As part of the University of the Nations, an international Christian university, he led multiple six-month bilingual discipleship programs and wrote the English-German leadership textbook *Ambassador*. He has been the guest speaker of numerous seminars about principles of Christian counseling and provided counsel to those seeking freedom from occult ritual abuse. Native to Switzerland, he moved to the United States and earned his Doctorate in Christian Philosophy with the Christian Leadership University. His book, *Celebrating the Feasts of Israel* testifies of his passion to see Christians grounded in the Word of God, personally experience Christ's love, and live victoriously. Today he resides in Seminole, Florida with his wife and two children.

Dr. Werner Sonderegger and his family

CPSIA information can be obtained
at www.ICGtesting.com
Printed in the USA
LVHW070502310819
629464LV00001B/1/P